Drop

Navigating the Waters of Life
Through God's Love

Lisa C. Whitaker

Books Publishing

... *Erkamka na Adonai is Hebrew for I love you, Lord* - Psalm 18:1

Name: Lisa C. Whitaker
Title: Dropping Anchor, Navigating the Waters of Life Through God's Love
Identifiers: ISBN: 978-1-952369-47-6
LCCN: 2021904533
Subjects: 1. Religion/General
2. Religion/Christianity/Personal Growth
3. Religion/Christianity/General

Cover Designer Bob Ousnamer
Anchor Image drawn by TJ Braden
Author photo by Lisa Haislet, 2019, Beverly Shores IN

Published by EA Books Publishing, a division of Living Parables of Central Florida, Inc. a 501c3

EABooksPublishing.com

ACKNOWLEDGMENTS

To my God, who has been so faithful in guiding me through all these waters of life and for giving me the stories to tell. To you I give all the glory!

To my children, Talor, Kyle, Aaron and Ethan, know that God has used you mightily in my life. It was through your lives many of the lessons were learned and my life stories were written. You four hold very special places in my heart both now and forever. I love you infinity!

To my husband, Steve, thank you for sticking with me through all the ups and downs in this life. I couldn't have picked a better partner to sail through life with. Here's to the next adventure.

To my prayer warriors in my Growth Group at Liberty Bible Church, I can't thank you enough for your prayers and support. You have no idea how many times I wanted to give up but your continual asking where I was in the writing process and your prayers of encouragement kept me going forward. Gil Cook, you are tenacious and I love you for it!

To Karen Wagner, my sister in Christ, I cannot even begin to thank you for your encouragement and support in this writing project. When I wanted to give up, you pushed me to continue. When I needed to cry, you listened and loved. When I was fearful, you helped me to straighten my crown and move forward in confidence. Karen, you are a treasure! Coffee and cheese curds any day!

Finally, to my Publisher, Cheri Cowell, you will never know how the words spoken to me on our first few phone conversations impacted me. When I shared my fears, you shared your experience. Your vulnerability in sharing with me your story was exactly what I needed to hear to take that next step. Thank you so very much for your wisdom and your promise to walk me through this process.

CONTENTS

Introduction   1

Part I   **Learning to Navigate**   2
Chapter 1   Setting Sail   3
Chapter 2   Love — The Stronghold   16
Chapter 3   What Is our Anchor?   35
Chapter 4   Knowing Your Anchor is
Dropped   48

Part II   **Waters of Life**   61
Chapter 5   Smooth Sailing   62
Chapter 6   Dry Docked   72
Chapter 7   High Seas   83
Chapter 8   Still Waters   98

Part III   **Compass Due North**   115
Chapter 9   Looking to the Horizon   116
Chapter 10   Final Destination   126

Personal Reflection   146
Invitation to Pray   161
Endnotes   162
About the Author   165

INTRODUCTION

Where are you in the journey of your life? Are you smooth sailing or are you in a battle of survival on the high seas of a major storm? Are you in dry-dock experiencing maintenance work or are you sitting in still waters, waiting, with no current or wind to move you? Every one of us will travel through these waters of life at some point and what you choose to take with you on your life's journey could mean life or death. I am talking about an anchor. We all will hook our life to something as a way of getting through life situations, but there is only one anchor strong enough to save. There is only one anchor that is sure and firm, one that gives strength and courage to your trembling heart. There is only one anchor that can give wings to your soul so it can soar even in the face of the fiercest adversity.

Come set sail with me and learn how this anchor, found in the awesome power of God's love, can be the instrument that gives you security, peace, and joy for your journey to your final destination, where you will drop your anchor for the last time. Home.

PART I

LEARNING
TO
NAVIGATE

CHAPTER 1

SETTING SAIL

It came today. The letter my youngest son was praying for and the one I was praying would never come. The letter began, "Dear Ethan, I am pleased to offer you an appointment to the United States Naval Academy as a member of the Class of 2018." My eyes blurred with tears and my heart began to pound in my chest. I couldn't continue to read the rest. I closed my eyes. "Lord, how could this be happening? I thought we talked about this, God! I specifically remember asking you to close the door on this opportunity!" On January 13, 2014, God and the Department of Navy set my son and me on a new course in life that I had not wanted. Despite my attempts to persuade him to choose "normal" college, Ethan's heart was set on something different, something bigger.

It all began in December 2013 when my son, Ethan, received not one, but two letters of nomination to the United States Naval Academy from one Congressman and one Senator. I understand most parents would be thrilled, but in all honesty, this was not what I wanted for my son.

I was thinking and feeling with my "Mom" senses, which told me this was a very dangerous move. Ethan had not even started at the Academy and the "what if's" were already circling like a buzzard over roadkill. What if he is severely injured, losing limbs, or disfigured? What if he comes back with his mind in utter torment from his experiences (PTSD)? What if he is killed or captured and tortured? Ethan hadn't even started school and I had him on the front lines of some horrific battle raging in some remote country far away from home. Oh yes, my brain had jumped on the "what if" train and that train was speeding down a one-way track on its way to Destructionville. I couldn't get past the thought that after four years of school, he would be serving our country for seven to ten years, possibly more, and potentially be put in harm's way. With so much unrest in the world today this was utterly frightening for me. Ethan was being recruited to swim for the University of Michigan, where his other two brothers attended. Truthfully, that's where I wanted him, as if by being there he would be completely safe from danger.

The tie that bound mother and son together began to stretch and pull. My emotions were at war with each other as I looked upon his joyful face. I could see the total excitement that lit up his eyes and stretched across his face, the sheer pride that he had made the cut. I knew from the information packet we received from the Academy that only twelve hundred young men and women would be selected and that year approximately eighteen thousand applied. I knew how difficult it was to get accepted to the Naval Academy in Annapolis, and what an honor it was to get that post, but my heart ached as fear invaded the deepest reaches of my soul. We had always taught Ethan to have courage, to put others before self and to have honor in what you do and now, I was faced with letting him live this out.

From the time we take our first breath in this world, we all embark on a voyage that takes us through many different waters. Sometimes the waters are calm and smooth but sometimes we find ourselves in terrifying high seas. Whether it's a devastating diagnosis from the doctor, the loss of a loved one, a broken relationship, the loss of a job, a child entering the military, or some other difficult circumstance, they will come. We may think we can control our lives to the point where we won't experience those high seas, but without a doubt, a time will come when the winds pick up and the waves will build to the point that they threaten to drown you. The question is, "what anchor do you use to try and secure yourself when those terrifying circumstances arise?"

The seas of my life were beginning to build. The alert rang out through my mind, "ROUGH SEAS AHEAD, BRACE YOURSELF!" This military thing was going to happen. There was nothing I could do to stop it. I had a choice to make here. I could allow myself to be tossed about on the high seas of doom and gloom, frozen in perpetual fear or I could drop my anchor in the stronghold of God's love. I chose the latter. Choosing this did not mean I would not have to endure the emotional highs and lows of my upcoming journey, but there was peace in the middle of it everywhere I turned. When we are faced with the unexpected, God's plan for our lives and that of our kids is enough to turn that uncertainty we feel around to a hopeful expectation. Our role is to be obedient to what we know of God and trust him for the rest.

In the days and months ahead, I learned a lot about the Navy. I also delved into Scripture searching for answers to how I would deal with the journey ahead. Every day, I would read God's word, searching for peace and comfort for the many emotions and questions I had. I can remember asking God how I was going to endure the next seven to ten years of my life with a son serving in our country's military. As if he had been waiting for me to ask, that day's Scripture included Hebrews 6:18-19. "God did this so that, by two unchangeable things, in which it is impossible for God to lie, we who have fled for refuge might have strong encouragement to hold fast to the hope set before us. We have this as a sure and steadfast anchor of the soul, a hope that enters the inner place behind the curtain." The first part of this Scripture tells us, "God did this." What did God do, you ask? The answer is found in the preceding verse, 17. It says, "God wanted to make the unchanging nature of his purpose very clear to the heirs of what was promised, so he confirmed it with an oath." God's whole nature is unchanging. He is the same yesterday, today and tomorrow and all his promises are unchanging. You don't have to be concerned that He will up and change his plans. To give us (his heirs) confidence in this, he confirmed it in an oath. This oath was made in God's name and it can be trusted because God is truth; it is "impossible for God to lie."

You may be asking, "who are the heirs and what is promised to them?" The answer is anyone who puts their faith in Jesus and accepts him as their Savior. The promise to the heirs is an eternal home with him in heaven. You see, the promise God made that gives his heirs hope came in the person and saving work of Jesus Christ on the cross. It is his life, death and resurrection. This hope Jesus gives us is an anchor that provides stability, security, and offers acceptance for those who believe and have placed their faith in him. It grounds our soul no matter what happens to us on this earth.

What's funny is that I have read the book of Hebrews so many times, but I never remembered the word "anchor" being used until now. It is so like God to flip on the "aahaa light" just when I needed it. A son in the Navy; the word "anchor" to describe the tool I was to use to get through the rough seas that lay ahead. All I can do is giggle and thank God for his never-ending love. It didn't stop there though. In the English Standard Version Bible I sometimes use, I caught sight of a little box at the bottom of the page called "Did You Know." In this box it said, "The safety of sailors depended greatly on a ship's anchor. Without it, the likelihood of shipwreck increased dramatically. The anchor therefore became an important emblem of hope and stability for early Christians." [1]

This Hebrews passage is the first time in the Bible that the image of the anchor is used to bring together the idea of hope through the work of the cross. Those early Christians adopted this symbol as an image of safety and steadfastness. The Apostle Paul was one who used the idea of an anchor in his writings. First Corinthians 15:58 says, "Therefore, my beloved brothers, be steadfast, immovable, always abounding in the work of the Lord, knowing that in the Lord your labor is not in vain" (ESV). Though he doesn't use the term "anchor" in his words, the image is portrayed in the idea of being steadfast and immovable. Paul also used the image again in Ephesians 4:14 when he talks about becoming mature and "attaining to the whole measure of the fullness of Christ." When Christians work together to build each other up in their faith of Jesus Christ, the Son of God, then as Paul says, "we will no longer be infants, tossed back and forth by the waves, and blown here and there by every wind of teaching and by the cunning and craftiness of men in their deceitful scheming." The idea of the "anchor" is seen in the maturity of a Christian to be able to stand firm, to be anchored in their faith, when the winds of adversity kick up.

When I finished reading the Scriptures God had for me that day and started meditating on them, something else began to infiltrate my mind. Even with all the thoughts that had been circling in my head, I knew two things without a doubt. One, Jesus loves me enough that he died for me, and two, it is not in God's nature to lie (Hebrews 6:17-18). If God cannot lie, then that means all his promises, everything he has ever written or spoke is truth. I can anchor myself in that with sheer confidence! As I began to process all of this, God brought to my mind all my "what if" questions but he gave them a new perspective. He changed my "what if" to "even if." "Even if" Ethan is injured in some way, "even if" Ethan comes back with a fractured mind, "even if"

Ethan is captured, God assures me he would be right in the middle of it because he promised he would "**never** leave or forsake us." "Even if" Ethan is killed God has promised that his soul is safe because Ethan has placed his faith in Jesus. Nothing will be able to separate Ethan from God's love! God promises this and if he promises this and he can't lie, it is truth! If this is truth, God then says, "what can mortal man do to you?" In other words, if he cannot lie, and he has promised to never be separated from us, then why would I worry about what can happen on this earth? What settled in my heart was the confidence that "even if" any of these things happened to Ethan, I would not lose him. I would know exactly where he was: anchored in the palm of God's hand. This truth is enough for me. Now, when I say this, it doesn't mean that if something did happen to our son, I wouldn't be devastated. Of course, I would be. I'm his mom! However, I am confident that God, in his promises, would surround me with his peace as he begins to heal my broken heart. I am confident that what God promised means I would see Ethan again one day. God's desire for us is that, amid the unforeseen, we would place our faith, hope, and trust in him alone.

Anchor. What is an anchor exactly? I decided to do a little research on anchors, starting with the idea of what an anchor is. To paraphrase the definition of an anchor, it is "an object, usually of metal attached to a ship or boat by a cable or rope. This object has sharp hooks, or flukes, that will dig into the floor of a body of water to hold the ship or boat firmly in position. I know most people do not like Wikipedia, but I love how they listed their definition of an anchor as "a device, normally made of metal, used to connect a vessel to the bed of a body of water to prevent the craft from drifting due to wind or current." [2] The bed of a body of water would be considered a stronghold or a place of security and yes, that's what I need! I need to be connected to a stronghold to keep from drifting or being shipwrecked during this voyage over the next several years.

Now that I knew what an anchor was, I decided to google anchors in terms of the US Navy. What I found boggled my mind. The USS Dwight D. Eisenhower (an aircraft carrier) has two anchors. Each anchor (just the anchor itself) weighs 60,000 pounds! Each anchor is then attached to a chain that is 1,082 feet in length where each link in the chain weighs 365 pounds (keep in mind there are 2 chains). The total weight for each anchor is 735,000 pounds! WOW!! These two anchors can secure this vessel that has a displacement of 95,000 tons, 4.5 acres of flight deck, houses approximately 60 aircraft, and is about the size of a twenty-four-story building from keel to mast. [3] My vessel, the "USS Lisa Whitaker," needs a strong anchor, one that will rival this one.

No wonder the anchor became the emblem of hope and stability for Christians. The use of the anchor gives us a picture of strength and confidence, which is how the Bible describes hope. Biblical hope is the confident expectation of what God has promised. Biblical hope is seen as past, present and future. We were saved the moment we put our faith in Christ. That is its past. Hope is present because we are being saved through our sanctification, the process in which our life is changing and growing in our new faith, becoming more like Christ. Finally, Biblical hope is future. Though God is at work in our life, making changes as he grows us, we have not yet received the full benefit of salvation. The full benefit of our salvation will come when Christ completely establishes his new kingdom. This is our future hope of our future home. The stability and strength of our hope are in God's faithfulness to deliver on his promise. This hope steeped in God's strength can confidently guide us in his truth so our compass can keep pointing in the right direction. The direction of home.

King David paints a wonderful picture of the strength found in placing our hope in God. In Psalm 62:5-8 he says, "Find rest, O my soul, in God alone; my hope comes from him. He alone is my rock and my salvation; he is my fortress; I will not be shaken. My salvation and my honor depend on God; he is my mighty rock, my refuge. Trust in him at all times, O people; pour out your hearts to him for God is our refuge." I love this imagery of God. He is a rock, a mighty rock, a fortress, a refuge and he saves. In him we will not be shaken. It's a picture of being secure; firmly held in a stronghold. It's the image of an anchor.

In life, there is no other anchor that is stronger and able to secure and give us hope than that of Christ's love. When God created man, he fashioned us with a homing beacon for the hope we have in Jesus. When we decide to follow something or someone other than what this beacon points us to (Jesus), our search for purpose, security, wellbeing, or even our identity in life will never be obtained.

We will always be frantically reaching for something that cannot give us what we so desperately want during the storms of our life: peace and a sense of security and hope.

Real hope is not just a thought we have when we are in need of something, such as when we say, "I hope I get this job, or I hope I don't die from this sickness. Real hope is not a wishful thought or something we think should happen so the end result will be fair such as when we say "I hope he is arrested for breaking into my car." When hope is used in this way, its strength is in the power of the person's wish. Think back to those anchors on that Navy ship. As strong as they are, they cannot stop a hurricane from coming, they cannot confidently provide life in the face of death. Do you want to know how strong our true anchor is? It can restore life from death (John 11:38-44). It can move mountains (Isaiah 40: 3-4), calm the torrent winds and raging seas with a single word (Mark 4:39), and it can make the evil forces run for the hills (Mark 5:8-13). Do you believe putting faith in a person's wish can achieve any of these? Real hope comes only from one person and that person is Jesus. He is the anchor that holds. He is the One who can take our desperation and turn it into a calm and content heart. He is the One who can pick us up and mend whatever is broken in our life, while giving us his peace at the same time. He is the only One that can give us boldness, confidence, security and assurance in the face of any circumstance through our hope in him.

God's love is the anchor I have chosen to secure me all the days of my life, wherever my journey takes me, and whatever the waters look like during that journey. I can confidently choose this because he promises he can hold me no matter what, and as I said before, it is not in his nature to lie! This hope, and this knowledge of Christ are great motivational forces that keep me striving to be all God wants me to be. I can stand firm in what God wants me to be because of who I am anchored in. In Philippians 3:12, the Apostle Paul says, "I press on, that I may lay hold of that for which Christ Jesus has also laid hold of me." Jesus had laid hold of Paul through his sovereign grace. As a result, Paul is able to press on to lay hold of the hope of all Christ had promised him through the finished work on the cross, his salvation. Paul understood the inspiring energy that encourages a person to grab onto the hope set before us. The energy comes, as our Hebrew passage says, from knowing God's promise and his oath and the fact that they are unchangeable. This should be a great encouragement for us as well to look beyond the unexpected turns in life and hold fast to the hope of a future set before us and never letting go of it.

What anchor do you use when the waves begin to rise? When you stand before your Doctor and hear the "C" word, where does your hope lie? When your spouse says, "I want out," where does your hope lie? When your boss gives you the pink slip, where does your hope lie? When you stand beside the grave of a beloved child, where does your hope lie? When your child tells you he or she is entering the military, where does your hope lie? This real hope we have in Jesus is confident. It's confident because it is based on his power and not ours. Are you confident in the anchor you use to secure your heart and soul? Does the person or thing that you place your hope in work?

HEBREWS 6:18-20 (NIV)

"God did this so that, by two unchangeable things in which it is impossible for God to lie, we who have fled to take hold of the hope offered to us maybe greatly encouraged. We have this hope as an anchor for the soul, firm and secure. It enters the inner sanctuary behind the curtain, where Jesus, who went before us, has entered on our behalf."

CHAPTER 2

LOVE – THE STRONGHOLD

In July 2006, our eldest child, Talor, received a full scholarship to swim for Washington State University. We were so proud of Talor and her accomplishments both in the pool and in the classroom, but WSU? It's very far away! (We lived in Indiana). Despite our ploys as parents to discourage her from going there, she continued to put WSU at the top of her list. Why can't kids just listen to their parents? Looking back, I am so glad she did not listen to the rantings of her earthly parents, in what were generated through fear. Instead Talor followed her heart, and the leading of her heavenly parent who was telling her his plan for her life was pulling her to the great state of Washington.

My husband and I decided to pray hard about this opportunity before us. God answered every concern we had with a solution. First was the obvious, the cost of attending a school so far away. The solution: the offer of a full ride scholarship.

Second was the crime rate in Pullman, WA. The solution came with an article my husband found that listed Pullman as having nearly zero crime. [4] Understandably, Pullman is in the middle of nowhere. In fact, when Talor and I went to visit the school, we were amazed at the wide, open and rolling hills, otherwise known as the Palouse. From the time you leave Spokane (where you fly into), until you reach Pullman, an hour and twenty-minute drive, you can almost count on one hand the number of houses or buildings. So, an important thing to remember is to make sure you use the bathroom at the airport before leaving Spokane or you will be looking for a tree if the need arises. I will say though, Pullman, Washington is a beautiful small town in which the town itself loves and supports their Cougars. The final concern, the straw that opened our eyes to the fact that this is where God wanted our daughter, was what if something happened to Talor? She would be so far away that it would take too long to get to her. A plane ride from here to Spokane is about 4 hours plus an hour and a half car ride from the airport to Pullman. Solution? Very dear friends of ours from our church informed us that their daughter had accepted a professorship starting that year at, you guessed it, Washington State University. She and her family would be living just off campus and would be more than willing to take Talor in and be there for her when we couldn't.

With our concerns covered by solutions, we had no other argument to persuade Talor not to go to Washington State. And so, she went. As Talor settled into Pullman, our friends helped her find a church home that she could attend during her four years there so she could stay connected to the body of Christ for fellowship and growth.

Why do I tell you this story? Because, it shows how much God loves us even in the simple things like making a decision on which school to attend. It shows that when you choose to anchor your heart and soul in his love, when we have concerns, we can take them to God, and he is faithful to remove them and show you the path he has mapped out for you. I must pause here to say it is important that you have your eyes open to the solutions God provides. It took me a while to finally comprehend that there were no more concerns standing in our way. I had been so sure that Talor should not go so far away from home that I had put blinders on when God provided the solutions. It was my husband who grasped it first and then began to convince me. If God loves to provide solutions to the simple or small concerns in our life, imagine what he does for the big ones!

In Genesis 41:32 God says, "The reason the dream was given to Pharaoh in two forms is that the matter has been firmly decided by God, and God will do it soon." This answered our questions about how we can know for sure if what we are facing is God's plan. Three solutions for our concerns for Talor answered, two letters of nomination and one letter of acceptance to the Naval Academy for Ethan. When God shows up and confirms to you a second time or more, in a firm way, you will know whatever you are facing is his plan. Second Corinthians 13:1 says, "This will be my third visit to you. Every matter must be established by the testimony of two or three witnesses." Then in Judges 6:36-40, God completes two tests using a fleece to confirm his promise to save Israel by Gideon's hand. In Genesis 37:5-10, Joseph had two dreams of the same kind indicating what God's plan was to come. Peter, in Acts 10:16, had a vision three times which showed him God did not consider anything he had made to be unclean. It was God's confirmation to Peter of his plan for Peter to gather with the Gentiles. The Bible has many instances where God confirms his plans in multiples.

Let me tell you that even though we were absolutely sure this was God's plan for our daughter, there were many tears on the weekend we took our daughter to school her freshman year. We had taken our three boys and even my father-in-law out to Washington to help get our daughter settled into her new life and to get a feel for the area for future visits. Some of us got busy cleaning her tiny dorm room while others in our group explored the rest of the dormitory. Then there were countless trips to Walmart to get all the necessary dorm items, such as bedding, storage containers, decorations, food, and the list goes on. We visited the natatorium (the indoor pool) and met the coach, for whom Talor would be swimming. We eventually toured the campus from top to top (I don't think there are any "downhills" on campus! I only remember all the uphills!). The weekend flew by and before I knew it, the final night came. We would be leaving the next morning to travel back to Indiana but without our daughter. That night before we were to depart Washington to come home, my husband and I sat up late and cried. Steve, my husband, finally said, "tomorrow will be hard for all of us, but we need to be strong for Talor." I shook my head in agreement while the tears ran down my cheeks. There was no sleep that came for me that night. In the morning, we all met for breakfast at the local Denny's restaurant before saying our goodbyes and as we all joined hands to pray, my husband's voice broke and the tears came. So much for being strong! I cracked open an eye to look at those around the table and noticed that all three boys had an eye cracked open looking at their dad, a look of shock covered each face. They had never seen dad cry before. My father-in-law's chin was quivering, urging the tears to break free and Talor had already lifted the flood gates to allow her tears to flow. I was so touched by the love my husband had for our daughter and I knew how his heart was overcome with sadness at the thought of leaving his "little girl" by herself, in a place far from home. My heart followed suit and in no time, I too began to choke back the tears. I, however, was determined to hold it together as we had agreed the night before.

We stood in front of her dormitory, each one of us giving a hug and saying goodbye, but when it was my turn, I could not pull my arms from around her neck. The tears were brimming and threatening to overflow. I could hardly speak; I just wanted to hold her forever. The car ride back to the airport was so quiet. Everyone was reflecting on their conversations and goodbyes with Talor. Life at home will be different without her there. We boarded the flight home, and I remember looking out the window as we lifted off seeing Washington shrink as the plane climbed higher. The idea of being strong went right out that same window. I turned to my husband with flooded eyes and sobs that came unhindered and told him I thought I was having a heart attack. The pain in my chest was undeniable. The solution? Take this hurt to the only one who could fix it. I cried all the way home, I'm sure the flight attendants must have thought someone close to me had died. Though my heart was heavy, I did feel God's presence. I did have confident peace that she would be okay. God would protect her and guide her these next few years, after all, this was his plan for her. I had to trust him with her, no matter what came down the road. My anchor had to rest securely in the promises God has made to me, knowing he cannot lie or change his mind.

Talor has been out of college a few years now and I can say without a doubt that Washington State University was indeed the best place for her. God was faithful! I look back and imagine my Father with a gentle smile as he lovingly took me by the hand and, prying my fingers off of Talor's life, provided all that was needed to assure me of his plan for our daughter. He allowed me to endure the pain of letting go, but he also provided the peace that gave me the encouragement needed to open my tightly gripped fingers from my daughter's future. Because of the love we had for our daughter and despite how much it hurt to watch her spread her wings and leave our home, we had to let her go and begin to make her own decisions in life, to live out the plan God had prepared for her. As her parents, we will always be there for her when she calls for advice, for wisdom, or a loving word of encouragement and comfort, but she now had to make her own way in life. When we release our grip on our kids' lives, God reminds us of the sure and firm anchor we have in his love that proves to be trustworthy and would remain so no matter what comes over the horizon.

Are you connecting the dots of how God looks on you as his child? How he provides for every detail in your life? Let me tell you another story of a father who had to also let a child go even though he knew the pain that his son would endure all for the sake of others who were so undeserving. The ultimate display of love and the birth of a living hope began thousands of years ago in the tiny little town of Bethlehem. Yes, I know, you've heard the story or have seen the pictures of baby Jesus with his parents in the stable at Christmas-time. Have you ever really thought about the story though? Ever considered what it has to do with you? The truth is, it has everything to do with you and me!

Do you know that back when God created this world and all that was in it, his desire was to create man in his own image as a way to show his own glory? That's where Adam and Eve came in. God's love for them was so great that he drew close to them, walked with them, and conversed with them. They lived in God's presence. Genesis 3:8 says Adam and Eve "heard the sound of the Lord God walking in the garden in the cool of the day . . ." God called out to them when they hid themselves, "where are you?" (ESV). You see, up until Satan had entered and deceived them, Adam and Eve enjoyed the abundance of love and companionship every day with our Creator in a place God designed for them that was described as a sanctuary. As much as

God loved Adam and Eve, he had created them to have the ability to choose to love God or not; this is what he called "free will." That love never ended for God but when Adam and Eve betrayed God's trust, a great divide was created so man could no longer be with God as it was in the beginning.

Sin cannot cohabitate with God and sin most definitely had entered the world. Solution? God had to set a plan in motion that would bridge this divide so that he could bring together the ones he so loves back to a place where they could once and for all be together as he originally intended. How could this be accomplished? Well, a price had to be paid for sure. According to God's laws, "the wages of sin is death . . ." (Romans 6:23), so someone had to die to pay the penalty of sin. It should have been Adam and Eve, who committed the original sin. It should be you and me for the sins we commit on a daily basis, but God, who so loved the world, decided he would send his son to die in the place of Adam and Eve and to die in the place of you and me (John 3:16). How do we know this was his plan? How did he confirm it? What did we say before? "Every matter must be established by the testimony of two or three witnesses" (2 Corinthians 13:1). Who were the witnesses? Actually, there were many, but some of the big players were Elijah, Jeremiah, and John the Baptist. God had called each of these men to testify to God's plan to send Jesus as the Messiah. Two times God confirms in a clear declaration that Jesus is his son. The first time was at Jesus' baptism in Matthew 3:16-17 and the second time was at his transfiguration in Matthew 17:5.

Romans 5:18-19 shows us how this plan of God's works. "Therefore, as one trespass led to condemnation for all men, so one act of righteousness leads to justification and life for all men. For as by the one man's disobedience (Adam) the many were made sinners, so by the one man's obedience (Jesus) the many will be made righteous" (ESV). The one trespass (sin) that led to condemnation for all men was Adam and Eve's decision to disobey God in the garden. The one act of righteousness that led to justification and life for all men was Jesus' obedience to the plan of his Father, whereby he would die on the cross to pay the penalty for all.

Oh, talk about love! Truth be told, this love bewilders me sometimes, especially when I see the hateful things some people do. Let me pause here for a moment. I can hear someone grumbling about the unfairness that we should be found guilty for something Adam did. Think about this though. Have you ever lied or deceived someone? Have you ever talked bad about someone behind their back? Have you ever kept something that wasn't yours? Have you ever thought about someone, other than your spouse, in a lustful way? If you answered "yes" to even one of these, in God's eyes, you are guilty of sin. You are cut from the same cloth as Adam and you have been born into Adam's family. Fortunately for us, God, knowing the hateful, sinful things people were going to do, (mine included), still offered up his one and only son so these same people will have a way to be with God forever if they so choose. We are all powerless to obtain life on our own, "but God demonstrates his own love for us in this: While we were still sinners, Christ died for us" (Romans 5:8).

We all fall into temptation, even after we have chosen to follow Christ. We still say things we should never say or behave in ways that expose our sinful nature. We even entertain wrong thoughts and desires, but God's solution covers it all and he is quick to forgive if we ask him (which we should). God offers us a chance, through the gift that came after Adam's downfall, to exchange our guilt for forgiveness. This gift is Jesus and through him we have the opportunity to change course and be born into his family, a family destined for eternal life. It is our choice, our decision to make. If we do nothing, we will stay in the family line that leads to death, but if we choose Jesus we will be welcomed with love and grace into the family that gives life.

There was a period when Jesus (the Son of God), just before he was betrayed into the hands of those who would condemn him to death, asked his

Father if there was another way to accomplish his plan. Jesus knew what the coming days would bring. The rejections, beatings, floggings, the nails and the cross and then ultimately the period where God the Father had to turn away from his own son as he took on your sins and mine (remember sin cannot cohabitate with God). In Matthew 26:38 Jesus told his disciples "my soul is very sorrowful, even to death . . ." and he wanted them to watch out for him while he went to pray. In verse 39, Jesus asked God "if it be possible, let this cup pass from me; nevertheless, not as I will, but as you will." Finally, in verse 42, Jesus once again said to his Father, "if this cannot pass unless I drink it, your will be done" (ESV). Three times Jesus asked, and three times God confirmed it was his will, this was the plan.

Despite knowing the pain Jesus would endure, God had no other solution, and Jesus, despite knowing the same, was willing to pay our debt. All because of the love they had for us. Imagine the heart-wrenching sadness God the Father felt for his son, as he had to allow Jesus to walk this road. Imagine the brokenness God must have felt when he had to release his own son, whom he loved so dearly, to enter the bowels of hell to defeat death. We don't always know what is down the road for our kids when we let them chase their dreams, but God knows. God knew what his son would endure and yet he still let him go. Why? Because that is how much he loves you and me. "For God so loved the world that he gave his one and only Son, that whoever believes in him shall not perish but have eternal life" (John 3:16). God sent his son, the one whom he loves, to make a sacrifice of love so we can have a place in his Kingdom of love for eternity. The kicker is that we don't deserve it, and God knows that, but he gives us this wonderful, amazing gift anyway.

John continues in 3:17-18 saying, "For God did not send his Son into the world to condemn the world, but to save the world through him. Whoever believes in him is not condemned, but whoever does not believe stands condemned already because he has not believed in the name of God's one and only Son." It's the family line issue again. Don't believe in Jesus, and you stay in the family line of Adam, guilty. Believe in Jesus and you are adopted into the family line of Jesus, saved! Though this is a gift from God, it does require an action on our part. We must choose to receive it, to believe "in" it.

Do you love someone so much that you would endure the separation of God's presence to ensure that they would live? Would you subject yourself to horrendous torture and ultimately death for the one you love? How about for those who don't love you back? Romans 5:8 says, "God shows his love for us in that while we were still sinners, Christ died for us" (ESV). Knowing the sins that had been committed and the sins we would commit in the future, Christ was still willing to pay the price because of his great love for us. Even though he knew many would reject his love gift he still thought it worth it in order to save a people whom he loved.

Christ's death and his resurrection defeating that death bridged the gap that was created in the garden and that now stood between you and me and God himself. For those who believe and place their faith in the work of Jesus Christ who willingly fulfilled God the Father's perfect plan now have a permanent solution to a life that originally held condemnation. First Corinthians 15:20-23 tells us, "But Christ has indeed been raised from the dead, the first fruits of those who have fallen asleep. For since death came through a man (Adam), the resurrection of the dead comes also through a man (Jesus). For as in Adam all die, so in Christ all will be made alive (family lines again). But each in his own turn: Christ, the first fruits, then, when he comes, those who belong to him." The opportunity to belong to God is God's love gift to us. It is the one stronghold that God offers us that gives us the ultimate security in which we can drop our anchor and not be afraid of the high seas that surround us.

What do I mean when I use the term "stronghold?" In the Bible, a stronghold can be used to describe God or sin. King David writes about God as a stronghold in Psalm 18:1-3 saying "I will love

You, O Lord, my strength. The Lord is my rock and my fortress and my deliverer; my God, my strength, in whom I will trust; my shield and the horn of my salvation, my stronghold. I will call upon the Lord, who is worthy to be praised; so shall I be saved from my enemies" (NKJ). Being anchored in a stronghold of God is a good thing. It means having strength, security, and safety. A stronghold in a sin sense is not good. These are areas of our life built on the lies Satan tells. They are perceptions and intentions of the heart we hold on to that are against God. They affect our attitudes, emotions, and behaviors, and they hold us captive, keeping us from living and walking in the freedom that Christ has won for us. The Apostle Paul illustrates this for us in his letter to the Corinthians. He writes, "since the weapons of our warfare are not worldly but are powerful through God for the demolition of strongholds. We demolish arguments and every high-minded thing that is raised up against the knowledge of God, taking every thought captive to obey Christ. And we are ready to punish any disobedience, once your obedience has been confirmed" (2 Corinthians 10:4-6 HCSB). Proverbs 21:22 gives us a picture of what it is like for the believer when Christ enters the heart of a sinner and destroys all their former strong, misguided confidences. It says, "A wise man scales the city of the mighty and brings down the trusted stronghold." Jesus exposes and demolishes those lies Satan has you holding on to and replaces them with the strong and confident stronghold of himself and his promises.

I love the passage in 1 Peter 1:3-9! In this passage, Peter tells us we should "praise the God and Father of our Lord Jesus Christ" because "in his great mercy he has given us new birth into a living hope through the resurrection of Jesus Christ from the dead." You want something to get excited about, something that makes you jump up and down and shout at the top of your lungs? It is that Jesus is our "LIVING HOPE," he has established our good and perfect stronghold. When he arose from the dead after his death on the cross, we who choose to believe and trust in him are given an inheritance that as Peter says "can never perish, spoil or fade and it is kept in heaven for us" (1 Peter 1:4). Even though we have to endure some trials for the time we are waiting for our inheritance, it's okay! We can rejoice because these trials are making our faith stronger and more genuine and that will bring honor and glory to Christ. We can rejoice because while we endure these trials, we have a stronghold to anchor ourselves in that will keep us from shipwreck.

This living hope we have in Jesus is our sure and firm anchor. He is not like the 735,000-pound piece of metal we see attached to those Navy ships; He is so much more powerful! He is strong and mighty to save. He is our stronghold that secures our soul. Are you that confident in the place where you drop your anchor? Do you have the evidence of security in the place where you drop your anchor? If not, why do you continue to drop your anchor there?

Romans 5:1-2 says, "Therefore, since we have been justified by faith, we have peace with God through our Lord Jesus Christ. Through him we have also obtained access by faith into this grace in which we stand, and we rejoice in hope of the glory of God" (ESV). Christ's peace is such a treasure! We receive this treasured gift by trusting God during the midst of life's storms. Would you not love to be able to rejoice even when the seas of your life are so high? It is possible! It all depends on what anchor you have to secure your soul; what good and mighty stronghold is securing your soul. In the world we live in, it is such a normal thing to come up against conflicting or adverse circumstances and in fact, God says we shouldn't be surprised by them. However, he also tells us that when they show up, we can rejoice because he has overcome the world and these circumstances are going to produce great things in us. So, let me hear you! If you are circling in a sea of hardship right now and you have chosen to drop your anchor in the stronghold of Jesus Christ, our living hope, let's hear you say, "IT'S OKAY! God's got me! I am shielded by God's power.

My faith is being made stronger." Hold fast friend!

Paul David Tripp said, "What we're all searching for is hope that won't disappoint us, that won't leave us hopeless in the end. What are you asking of something when you place your hope in it? You're asking it to give you peace of heart. You're asking it to give your life meaning. You're asking it to give you purpose and direction. You're asking it to give you a reason to continue. You're asking it to help you get through difficulty and disappointment. You're asking it to free you from envy or anxiety. You're asking it to give you joy in the morning and rest at night" ("New Morning Mercies"). [5] Wow that's a lot to ask isn't it? So again, I ask you, where or in what are you placing your hope to secure your soul? What tool or anchor are you using? Do you have peace of heart? Does your life have purpose and meaning and direction? If you are being disappointed time after time, then perhaps it's because it's the wrong anchor or tool! Might you consider placing your hopeful heart in the hands of Jesus today? He's the only one who can fulfill all those things that you ask of your anchor.

John 3:16-18 (NIV)

"For God so loved the world that he gave his one and only Son, that whoever believes in him shall not perish but have eternal life. For God did not send his Son into the world to condemn the world, but to save the world through him. Whoever believes in him is not condemned, but whoever does not believe stands condemned already because he has not believed in the name of God's one and only Son."

CHAPTER 3

WHAT IS OUR ANCHOR

How many times have you found yourself on the high seas of a life situation and you're struggling to keep yourself above water? You can't seem to find a solution to calm the fear rising in your heart. You feel like the waves are going to overcome you. God tells us that all we have to do is ask him for the solution, to ask him for the wisdom on what to do. However, when we ask, we must do it in **faith**, with no doubting, "for he who doubts is like a wave of the sea driven and tossed by the wind" (James 1:5-6 NKJ). Believe me when I say, "it is not fun being in a place where it feels like the wind is playing badminton with your life."

We've been talking about the importance of using an anchor to secure us as we travel the different waters of life and we have learned that God's love is the one place where we can find peace and hope when we drop anchor. You may be asking though, "What is this anchor exactly? What does it look like?" Obviously, we don't carry around a 735,000-pound piece of metal in case we encounter rough waters.

If you look at a traditional anchor symbol, you

will notice there are two hook points that curve upward from either side of the stem of the anchor. These two points are what grab hold of a solid surface (usually the ocean bed) to provide stability and security. Our anchor also consists of two hook points. They are called faith and trust. The solid surface that they grab hold of is the hope we receive in the finished work of Jesus Christ on the cross, his love gift of eternal life. It's our stronghold. In other words, believers in Christ, who are righteous in God's sight (because they have placed their faith in Jesus), have a sure hope of future glory and life eternal. The neat thing is that as you look at the anchor, the "stem" that comes down to the two hook points is shaped like a cross. The cross is connected to the faith and trust hook points, which then secures itself in the hope (the solid surface or stronghold) given through the finished work of Jesus Christ on the cross and his resurrection. What a visual image this gives us!

The Bible refers to Christ as the "rock," but not just any rock, a "solid rock." Look at Psalm 18:2, "The Lord is my solid rock, my fortress, my rescuer. My God is my rock – I take refuge in him! – he's my shield, my salvation's strength, my place of safety" (CEB). Christ is all of this for us because of his death and resurrection, which defeated death once and for all. This death he defeated was to be sin's punishment for us, but now it is labeled "debt paid in full." This place of safety is our solid surface, our stronghold that we can drop our anchor into with confidence that it will hold. Jesus is our ultimate dwelling place, our hope that we are connected to through God's grace, through his love in sending his

Son to pay our debt of sin.

God has given us our solid surface to drop anchor in, but now it's our turn. How do we drop anchor? God's provision of our solid surface came through the cross (the upper part of the anchor) and our part, our action of dropping anchor comes through "faith" and "trust" (the hook points of the anchor). Every single, person on this earth puts their faith in something or someone. It may be your job, your spouse, the government or even yourself. These objects of faith will, apart from God, let us down. Every day we exercise acts of faith or trust in our life. As you go to sit down in a chair you trust the chair will hold you. Whenever you get in a car, you trust the car will get you to your destination. If you didn't, you wouldn't get in. When you step inside your home you flip a switch having faith the lights will come on.

So, what is faith? What is trust? Faith is when you have a complete trust or confidence in something or someone. You believe in it or in them with everything you have. Hebrews 11:1 says faith "is the assurance of things hoped for, the conviction of things not seen" (ESV). This is a description of what faith does. Faith looks at things hoped for as truth. Faith itself proves that what is unseen is absolutely authentic. Faith takes God at his word. In the book of Hebrews, chapter 11, the words, "by faith" or "through faith" were used twenty-four times. That's big! This chapter speaks of so many people who did amazing things through their faith in God that made an impact not only in their own lives but also in the lives of the generations to come. It's cool to think our name could be added to that list one day if we choose to live by faith.

Earlier in the year (2020) our church had a gentleman from Costa Rica come to speak briefly to us about where and how our "Thanksgiving Offering" we sent them was being used. I listened to him speak of having faith in God to provide for their needs and their ability to rejoice ahead of time in trusting that his help was coming. He summed it up saying, "Hope is the promise of a future that God gives us through Jesus Christ. Faith is the courage we have to dance in the present." I loved this! Did you connect with this too? What gives us the courage to dance in the present, no matter what is going on around us? The promise of a future that Christ Jesus gives us. It is our hope, and it is a certainty. Hebrews 10:23 says, "Let us hold fast the confession of our hope without wavering, for he who promised is faithful." How true it is that the faith we have in what God has given us allows us to rejoice in the here and now, no matter our circumstance.

According to *gotquestions.org*, the Hebrews' explanation of faith contains two aspects: intellectual assent and trust. Intellectual assent is believing something to be true. Trust is **relying** on the fact that the something is true. Remember the idea of trusting the chair to hold you? Intellectual assent is recognizing that a chair is a chair and agreeing that it is designed to support a person who sits on it. Trust is actually sitting in the chair. [6] Simply put, faith isn't merely believing something; faith is belief *plus* behavior. It is believing in something and taking action that is agreeable with what we believe.

With respect to our anchor, believing Jesus is God incarnate who died on the cross to pay the penalty for our sins and was resurrected is not enough. James 2:19 tells us even the demons believe in God and in those facts. We must personally and fully rely on the death of Christ as the atoning sacrifice for our sins. We must "sit in the chair" of the salvation Jesus Christ has provided; this is our "action" step of faith. This is saving faith. The faith God requires of us for salvation is belief in what the Bible says about who Jesus is and what he accomplished, and fully trusting *in* Jesus for that salvation (Acts 16:31).

Here is a kicker though. This faith in something "unseen" is not natural for us. It is more natural for us to worry or fear or try to control things ourselves. This faith in Jesus isn't something we create in ourselves. This faith comes to us as God's gift of grace. Ephesians 2:8-9 says, "For by grace you have been saved through faith. And this is not your own doing; it is the gift of God – not by works, so that no one can boast" (ESV). God not only creates in you the heart to believe and claim his gift of salvation, but he also creates in you the faith to really grab hold of it, to be able to live by it, to hold fast to it. Though this faith may start out small and weak, God will continue to work to build it in your life until this faith rules your heart without faltering.

When my first son, Kyle, was a freshman in high school, God gave me a little lesson in faith and trust. You see Kyle was an up and coming phenom swimmer. From the time he was ten years old he was breaking all kinds of records and making headlines in the local news. I knew God had given him a talent that he would use in some way. However, as Kyle headed into the Indiana High School State Championship his freshman year, there was such expectation placed on him by the media and by spectators to be the top contender. I, as his mother, became concerned. The pressure was building for Kyle to be totally and completely successful. I worried about what would happen if Kyle didn't deliver on those expectations. The newspapers are good at building you up, but they will be the first to tear you down when things go awry. I feared the disappointment not only from Kyle himself, but also from others who had placed such a faith in his ability. I was afraid of what that kind of let down could do to such a young man.

It wasn't that I didn't believe he could do it. But I was also realistic in the fact that there was a big difference in the physical stature of the senior boy who was his biggest competition in the 200 Individual Medley race and Kyle's yet to fully develop stature as a freshman. Simply put, Kyle's competition had "man muscles" and he was a very good swimmer in his own right. Next to him, Kyle looked like a little boy. It seriously looked like the David and Goliath story had walked out of the pages of the Bible and into the twenty-first century.

Before the finals race, I went to the bathroom and shut myself in a stall and let the tears fall. (On a side note, I have done a lot of praying in bathroom stalls. They are a good place to shut yourself off from others so you can pray). For me, when nervousness and anxiety build to a certain level, I know to go to a quiet and secluded place because the dam is about to break. I was an emotional mess. I lifted my concern to the One I knew who could provide peace.

There in the stall of the bathroom I heard, in my heart, God telling me he was going to do something amazing; I just needed to watch and see. I needed to believe in him. I needed to trust that what he spoke to me would come to fruition. I left that bathroom in peace and with full confidence God heard my request and was indeed going to do something amazing.

The enormous natatorium was packed, and the atmosphere was electric in anticipation of this next race. It was the race everyone had come to see. As Kyle walked out to his starting block, tears stung my eyes. I was so proud of him, but I knew his heart had to be thumping hard in his chest. When Kyle is really nervous, he gets these red streaks on his cheeks and at that moment they were visible even up in the balcony stands where we sat. Behind his block, Kyle bent down on his knee and bowed his head asking God for strength. This made my heart swell even more. Once again, I prayed for him. I prayed for God's strength and endurance for him. From the time his feet left the blocks, I never stopped praying, I never wanted to stop believing what I heard in the bathroom stall, but oh that which is natural for us to believe began to creep in.

After the butterfly portion of the race, Kyle and his opponent were almost even, but after the backstroke portion, Kyle fell behind. His opponent was known for his backstroke ability and he let the spectators know it as he flew down the lane picking up speed and putting distance between him and Kyle. By the time the breaststroke part ended Kyle had made up a little ground but now there were only two lengths of the pool left to complete. They turned into the last fifty yards of freestyle, and it looked as if Kyle was too far behind to catch his opponent. Spectators were already beginning to shake their heads in disappointment and the photographers on the pool deck were jockeying for the best position to get that winning shot at the end of the lane. My faith in what I thought God had spoken to me began to falter. I started to question God's words and what I heard in response was "watch and see. Trust me!" At that moment, I felt like the Dad in the Bible that had the demon-possessed son (Mark 9:14-24). The dad asked Jesus that "if he could do anything, take pity on us and help us," to which Jesus replied, "If you can? Everything is possible for him who believes." The dad then exclaimed, "I do believe; help me overcome my unbelief!" I wanted so badly to believe in what I heard God speak in my heart, but I needed him to help me overcome my unbelief.

As I continued to pray, Kyle made up a little ground on the first 25 yards of freestyle and as they turned into the last 25 yards, something happened. Kyle's opponent began to lock up. His arms suddenly looked as though they were moving in slow motion. Kyle shot off the wall and with all the strength he could muster he began to pick up speed. It was as if someone had flipped a switch to ignite the after burners of an engine. The gap between them began to close rapidly. Kyle's muscles seemed to have found new life, more strength, a new energy, like he was tethered to a bungie cord that was now recoiling. Every person in that natatorium was on their feet and the cheering was deafening. The tears were flooding my eyes and I was still praying although I was now doing it very loudly in the form of screaming as I jumped up and down. The finish line was coming so fast, but true to God's word, something amazing occurred. Kyle overtook his opponent just before the last five yards for the win.

I know you are thinking this is silly. It's a swim meet. But let me say God uses all kinds of situations in our lives to teach. Swimming is such a big part of my family's life so it's natural he would use that as a teachable moment. Jesus has a genius ability to use life analogies to teach. For example, the parable he told of the one lost sheep (Matthew 18:12). Those who tend sheep or livestock will understand his teaching. How about the parable of the vineyard owner (Mark 12:1-11)? Those that are growers of grapes or other plants will understand this teaching. These are just two of life's teachable moments. The Bible is full of them. The point being that Jesus uses so many different life illustrations to teach and he knows exactly which ones to use in each of our lives and at what times to use it. That day God used swimming to teach me about faith and trust. The fact that he spoke to me at all is important. We tend to limit ourselves in our thinking of how God can speak to us, but Scripture has shown that he can do it however and whenever he wants. Think about it. We have examples in the Bible where he spoke through dreams, with a still small voice, during the middle of the night, during funerals, while people were walking on the road, and in the middle of a storm. The list goes on. Why not in a bathroom stall at a swim meet?

Now, I would never presume to say God caused the other swimmer to lock up so Kyle could win, and

I could be taught a lesson. But it's possible that in God's omniscience he knew this boy would *choose* to go out way too fast in the front half of the race and as any swimmer could tell you, that could mean a death sentence for the second half of your swim. What I know for fact is that before Kyle's race, I sought God's help through prayer. Kyle, behind his starting block, bowed his knee and head in prayer. All our family watching prayed for Kyle. We all prayed specifically for his strength, endurance, and that God would give him the heart of a warrior. God's word says that, "if two of you agree on earth about anything they ask, it will be done for them by my Father in heaven. For where two or three are gathered in my name, there am I among them" (Matthew 18:19-20 ESV). What we ask of God though should be in accordance with his will and on that particular day, I believe it was. What I learned is that when God tells me he would do something, he will do it. It wasn't about Kyle winning or losing. It was about learning to trust God's word even when things look bad. It was about learning to let my faith in God's promises govern my heart without faltering, and I realized I needed to work on that. When our faith is placed in God, the Holy Spirit will begin to help us recognize God's voice, and his message at all times, no matter where we are and no matter our circumstances. The mere fact God wants to communicate with us at all, let alone teach and instruct us, causes me to be overwhelmingly joyful.

In Kyle's swimming career, he had many defeats, many of them were heartbreaking and they came even though we all had prayed, but the lesson during those circumstances was one of learning to still give God the glory. As Kyle ended his swimming career, I learned God loves me so much that he will not only give me unspeakable joy, but also teach me about faith and trust as he does it. My belief in the person of Jesus and his promises grew stronger and more confident just in that one lesson during Kyle's high school freshman year, but then God expanded on the lessons he taught me and he grew me in the ones I needed to learn and become stronger in as the years continued. Some of the lessons were born out of sheer turmoil and I can say those lessons were not only the hardest to learn but they were the ones that grew my roots in Christ the deepest.

Look at the story of David and Goliath. David, a young shepherd boy of only twelve or fifteen years old sat in his faith of his God because he had experienced God's power before while out in the fields tending his sheep. When King Saul told David he was just a boy and too young to fight a seasoned warrior in Goliath, David recounted to him the times when he fought off a bear and a lion all while under God's protection. He was confident his God would do the same with Goliath. When every man in the army was too afraid to face this nine-foot giant, David, rooted in his faith and trust in the only God who can save, went out and stood tall in confidence before a giant. His anchor was secure in God's power. Listen to David's words to Saul, "The Lord who delivered me from the paw of the lion and the paw of the bear will deliver me from the hand of this Philistine" (1 Samuel 17:37). David didn't waiver in his words. His words were "The Lord WILL do this." To everyone else, this situation looked bad for

David, but David was sitting in the chair of his faith. David wasn't boasting in anything he had done, he was giving credit where credit was due. He was giving God the glory.

"For by grace you have been saved through faith, and that not of yourselves; it is the gift of God, not of works, lest anyone should boast" (Ephesians 2:8 - 9). God's love gift to us is his grace, his promise of life eternal. We cannot do anything to earn this gift. All we need to do is accept it. Believe it. Trust it completely. "Sit in it." This is what our anchor looks like. We accept the hope God offers us as a gift, and we believe **in** it and we trust it with our whole heart and in full confidence. As Romans 5:5 tells us, "Hope does not disappoint us, because God has poured out his love into our hearts by the Holy Spirit, whom he has given us."

What does your anchor look like?

Ephesians 1:8-9 (NIV)

"For it is by grace you have been saved, through faith – and this not from yourselves, it is the gift of God – not by works, so that no one can boast."

CHAPTER 4

KNOWING YOUR ANCHOR IS DROPPED

Tears stung my eyes as the hospital technician finally revealed the fact that I had two babies growing inside my womb. Twins! My tears gave way to sobs as I contemplated how God could have allowed two more children to be born into a marriage that to some looked like it was struggling, but in my heart, I believed it was beyond that. In my heart, it was failing. Having more children was not something that was on my radar. I left the hospital distraught as fear began to ravage my heart. What will happen now? Will I end up being a single mother of four little ones and if so, how will I survive? I was a stay-at-home mom, but would I have to go back to work now and if so, who would take care of my kids? All these thoughts came crashing together in my mind and my sobs grew to an unrelenting volcano of tears.

My pregnancy became a long, difficult, and uncomfortable road. As the weeks went by and my stomach (and ankles) grew, I began to love these little ones. I knew God had to have a purpose for their lives, and I relished the idea that he was letting me be their Mom. The weeks turned into months and I began to slowly see a change in my marriage for the better. It was almost as if these babies were a healing thread stitching up the wounds present in my relationship with my husband. Hope formed on the horizon for our marriage. Now, let me stop here for a second and say that if your marriage is in a bad place, do not think by having a baby it will get better! I am saying here that *God chose* to use these babies as a vessel to bring healing to our marriage. This was God's plan not ours! Only he could know how these babies could bring healing.

Max Lucado said in his book, *Anxious for Nothing,* that "Times of despair and anxiety are not one-night storms; they can last for years. Tragedy does not adhere to the rules of convenience." Now I certainly do not think of having twins as a tragedy, but this event did come at a very inconvenient time of our lives as we saw it. Oh, and by the way, this storm was definitely not a one-nighter. In fact, those winds were beginning to pick up and the waves were starting to build. Unfortunately, I did not have my anchor in good working order at the time and the winds were causing me to lose the footing I had in my faith relationship with God. It was not securely anchored where it should have been, and it had become rusty and unused.

On June 6, 1995 my kidneys began to shut down and I was engulfed in pain. After I was rushed to the hospital by my Mom who was visiting at the time, my doctor made the decision to perform an emergency C-Section, afraid the babies were in danger. These two precious boys would be born seven weeks premature. At four pounds for one baby and four pounds and thirteen ounces for the other they made their way into the world letting everyone know they had arrived. They both had a few health issues to overcome as their lungs were not quite fully developed, but the doctors were confident they would make it. Placed in separate isolate beds with so many wires, tubes, and monitors attached to them, they struggled for a few weeks in the Neonatal Care Unit before coming home still attached to their heart monitors. Aaron, the smallest of the two, had to stay a bit longer than his brother, Ethan, as he had a more difficult time gaining weight. I spent day after day for several weeks driving back and forth to the hospital, trying to deal with the guilt of not being able to be present with both babies at the same time until finally, they both were home.

The storm we found ourselves in only got stronger and a lot more frightening over the next two months. One early morning, at two months of age, little Aaron stopped breathing. His heart monitor sounded the alarm, waking my husband and I from a much needed, peaceful sleep. As I swept into his room to reset the alarm, thinking the sensor around his chest had shifted or had become loose like it had a few times before, a voice in my head told me to stop and look closely at him. The first thing that caught my attention was how pale and colorless his little face was. My little boy had stopped breathing. I immediately snapped him up out of his bed and began CPR. It didn't take long to get him breathing again, but little did I know it would not be the last time I would have to do this.

After a call to our pediatrician, we thought we had a cause and a solution, but a few hours later Aaron stopped breathing again as my sister held him in her arms during her visit to our home. This time my husband immediately called 911 but as he dialed something came over me that said, "I'm in control, I can get our son to the hospital faster than an ambulance and as long as he was in my arms on the way he would be okay." My faith right at that point was in myself to save our son. That's where I was dropping my anchor. As we sped to the hospital to meet our doctor, Aaron continued to stop breathing. I cannot even begin to tell you what it is like to see the color drain from your child's face and see his small blue eyes glaze over as if the windows to his soul were closing. My tears are flowing just thinking about it.

Once we arrived at the emergency room our doctor met us with her staff of nurses and they quickly took Aaron out of my arms and placed him in a small isolate bed. The moment my arms were empty I felt my heart rip in two and a sudden terror filled the gap. It was the first time in my life I felt so completely not in control. Tears finally began to fall as if the flood gates had broken free. Gone was my confidence in my saving ability. Gone was my faith that Aaron would be okay. I was stripped bare of everything I had confidence in. My sure and firm anchor in Christ had been neglected over the years, so I didn't immediately turn to it, holding fast to it until Jesus gave me no other choice.

As God whittled away at my desire to be in control, allowing me to watch our son's chest cease to move time after time, an anger ignited deep down and rose with each episode. When would the end come? Why, God, were you doing this? How many times would the nurses be able to resuscitate him before his little body gave up? I was angry with God! First, he brings this little one into my life during an insecure time, and then he allows me to form an attachment to him, and to love him with my whole heart. Now he is just going to rip him away from me! Yes, the anger grew.

The next several hours became a wrestling match between me and God. I called him names and I told him I couldn't love a God that would do this. Just at the appointed time, my sister called to check in on us. I opened my mouth and out came a flood of hatred and bitterness that shocked her into silence. She did say one thing that struck a chord in my heart though. She said I was giving Satan a foothold into my life. Looking back, I didn't just give him a foothold, I gave him the "whole nine yards" of my heart. My sister admitted to me later that she hung up the phone and hit her knees, praying the hardest she has ever prayed.

I had not only failed to drop my anchor in the right place, I was allowing the waves to toss me around and push me under. After what seemed like hours, I became exhausted from the battle and I knew I would not survive this if I didn't make a change. This was the pivotal point. I began to feel the anger soften and the overwhelming desire to rest in Jesus' arms came crashing into my heart. The battle for my life was won. The prayers of so many had been heard by the Father and at his command Satan had to leave. At that very moment I fell to my knees and surrendered not only my desire for

control but also my son's life to God. I confessed to
God that I knew Aaron was ultimately his child and
if God's will was to take Aaron home that day, I
could do nothing but ask him to give me a mighty
strength to be able to stand up under it.

At long last my anchor that is sure and firm was
dropped and secured in God's amazing love where
it needed to be, and I was holding fast to it. It was
secure in the hope that I received from Jesus when
he offered the gift of eternal life. That hope assured
me that if Aaron went to be with Jesus that day, a
time would come when I would be able to hold him
in my arms again. An amazing peace enveloped my
whole being and I could feel God's presence
everywhere around me. It was like a warm blanket
wrapped around me, comforting and softening the
pain in my heart.

I felt like I had aged a thousand years as I slowly
made my way back to Aaron's little isolate room. As
I pushed open the doors to the Neonatal unit a nurse
quickly came striding up to me with a grin on her
face that stretched a mile long. In the few hours that
I had stepped away, the doctor had given Aaron
several units of blood due to a test that revealed a
lack of that life-giving liquid to pump his heart
efficiently. The nurse commented she had never
seen a baby turn around as fast as Aaron did in the
Neonatal Unit. His skin was the most beautiful
shade of pink! When I entered Aaron's private room
there on the back of the small isolate bed was a card
that read, "Be still and know that I am God." Though
I thought I had cried every tear possible already,
more of them stung my eyes as I read the card over
and over, the words resonating in the deepest

reaches of my heart. Where did this card come from? The nurses I talked to had no idea. Days later I found that a pastor from our church had come and prayed over Aaron while I was away wrestling with God, and he had placed that card there before he left. Of all the cards he could have chosen to leave behind it was the one with the most powerful words that would strengthen my anchor's hold, the words that would be planted and take root deep in my soul. God is in control and I had to be still and let him be!

There is a story in the Bible about a guy who was also living his life as if he was in control. The story of Absalom, King David's son, is an interesting one. When I read through his story, I can see so much of myself in the way he put stock in his own ability to control. Absalom at first glance had the markings of a great king. He had good looks, skill, position and the people loved him. Second Samuel 15:6 tells us that through flattery and deceit, Absalom "stole the hearts of the men of Israel." His desire was to oust his own father and become king himself. He was self-centered, doing what he wanted, when he wanted. He made decisions based on the advice of others and by his own accord. Absalom had not adopted his father's desire to seek out and follow after God. He never sought forgiveness but continued to run wild after the desires of his own heart. He crowned himself king while he was staying in Hebron and in Second Samuel 18:18 it says he built a monument to himself. Can you see the vanity and pride that were Absalom's anchor? As we said before, anchors secured in any other place, besides in the stronghold of God's love, fail every time. Absalom's anchor was no different. His anchor did not have the power to save. Absalom never realized the need for a stronger, surer anchor when his storm raged around him and it ultimately led to his destruction.

In the season of your life when you are trying to weather a major storm, one that seems to be throwing everything at you, including the kitchen sink, the only way to survive is to have a strong anchor to hold fast to, an immovable one. Do you have anything like this to cling to in your storms? It took me a while, but I finally realized I needed to secure myself in the belief that I had in what Jesus had accomplished on the cross. Up until this journey, I had believed everything I had read "about" Jesus, but when the rubber met the road, especially when it dealt with the possibility of losing a child, did I really have confidence "in" Jesus and his power and in his promises? When God started me down this road, I don't think I did, but that all changed when Jesus walked me through to the other end of the road. Again, I say that if God had taken Aaron that day, I would find joy in knowing that one day I would hold him again because this is the hope and assurance that my anchor in Christ gives. Yes, it would have taken time for my heart to heal from the loss, but my hope in a future reunion would still be present, it's what would sustain me for the time while I waited for that reunion to occur. That anchor, for those who have accepted Christ as their Savior, promises that we would all be together in paradise for an eternity.

James 1:2 says we are to "count it all joy when you fall into various trials" (NKJ). It doesn't say, "*if* you fall into trials," it says, "*when* you fall into trials." As I said in Chapter 1, you *WILL* have high seas in your life. It doesn't matter who you are. Why should we think of trials as joy though? James goes on to say in verses 3-4, "knowing that the testing of your faith produces patience. But let patience have its perfect work, that you may be perfect and complete, lacking nothing" (NKJV). In this passage, the term patience means more than just enduring difficulties. It includes the idea of standing fast under pressure, with a staying power that turns adversities into opportunities (NKJV Commentary).[8] By dropping your anchor in God's love, you will find "staying power" to help you endure the storm. You will not just endure it, but you will come out of it standing strong. You will find joy in the way that storm has perfected your faith even more as you wait for Christ to take you home to heaven.

We should always walk closely with God daily, so we can recognize the very minute we are in trouble and have our anchor dropped, securing us in the only stronghold that can save us. I should have had my anchor dropped in God's love long before the day Aaron had stopped breathing, but I rested too much in my own ability to effect change. That was a mistake and unfortunately, it probably won't be the last time I make that mistake, but I will be quicker next time to turn to that anchor and hold fast to it. Because of God's great mercy he not only gave Aaron life, but he also restored my marriage. Sometimes God must use intense situations in our lives to bring about a change in us and many times those situations are not one-time scenarios. Some of us are a little slow at learning what God is trying to do in our lives so he may have to keep at it until we do. In my case, I have been known to be slow as molasses in the learning department. But just as the passage in James that I previously shared with you said, I came out of this with a much stronger and mature faith in God. Trials are part of God's "good gifts" to his people, to strengthen them in their faith. He doesn't shelter us from the hard times of life because he knows we need them for our spiritual growth (Romans 5:3-5). So then, how can I not joyfully thank God for allowing this storm to pass through my life, for growing me in my faith that I'm sure I will need again later down the road?

Ask yourself, "When the storms darken my sky, how do I respond?" Do you see them as a "good gift," a tool, or a sign of God's love for you? Or do you doubt his goodness when they come and allow yourself to be tossed around and pushed under? James is telling us in Scripture that God uses these storms you face as a tool of his transforming grace. These momentary hard times are not in your life because God isn't watching or concerned with you, but he allows them because he loves you infinitely. He loves you enough to grow you and strengthen you.

I read a devotional, written by Paul David Tripp, where he said, "Right here, right now, God isn't working to deliver to you your personal definition of happiness. He's not committed to give you a predictable schedule, happy relationships, or comfortable surroundings. He hasn't promised you a successful career, a nice place to live, and a community of people who appreciate you. What he has promised you is himself, and what he brings to you is the zeal of his transforming grace." [9] He alone can "work things together for your good" (Romans 8:28). He alone can transform you, strengthen you, and give you the courage you need to stand in adversity.

Have you ever noticed how many "self-help" books and DVDs there are out there? The bookstores and online warehouses are full of them. There are so many because authors realize the despair people find themselves in on a daily basis. In a sermon our pastor delivered one Sunday, he said, "we are only a day away from despair." That stuck with me. We could be sailing along in calm beautiful waters with nothing but blue sky and fair winds when in the blink of an eye the waves will build, and the clouds will race in. It's time to batten down the hatches, drop anchor, and hold fast.

Sometimes we get so complacent with our lives sailing along without a care in the world that we fail to see the signs of the approaching storm. Absalom was operating in this way. The only thing he cared about was becoming king. He sailed along in his ambition to make this happen and failing to see the storm building on the horizon. Other times, there are no signs. The storms seem to come out of nowhere. The morning our son stopped breathing was a "blindside" storm for us. What is important to know is where to turn when the storms roll in, when and where to drop your anchor. Recognizing when you need to secure yourself to the stronghold that you have faith in. There is an old sailing term that the captain of a ship would yell out to his crew so they could prepare themselves for the impending danger of a storm. It is *"HOLD FAST!"* This term told the crew they needed to grab hold of the anchor ropes and hold on tightly. The anchor that we should "hold fast" to is the hope Jesus gives us through his finished work on the cross, his death, and resurrection.

So, I say to you, make sure your anchor is in good working order and that it is secured in the right place so when you need to "hold fast" to it, you can. Then as you are holding on, remember to "Rejoice always, pray without ceasing, give thanks in all circumstances; for this is the will of God in Christ Jesus for you" (1 Thessalonians 5:16-18 ESV)

James 1:2-4 (NIV)

"Consider it pure joy, my brothers, whenever you face trials of many kinds, because you know that the testing of your faith develops perseverance. Perseverance must finish its work so that you may be mature and complete, not lacking anything."

PART II

WATERS OF LIFE

CHAPTER 5

SMOOTH SAILING

I woke early to the sound of a soft rain on September 27, 1986. As I laid in bed, I let my mind drift to thoughts of the day ahead. I smiled. Joy began to well up in my heart. It was my wedding day. It didn't even bother me that it was raining on my wedding day. I have heard rain on a wedding day is a good thing. I look at it as a clean, fresh start in life as a married couple. Truthfully, I don't remember much else of the morning routine. I vaguely remember doing my make-up and my hair, though I know I did them myself. The only thing I can recall about that morning was feeling incredible joy. Once at the church, the clouds dissipated, and the sun began to shine. I thought God had made everything new and perfect just for me. My dress hugged my body and my veil softly fell over my face as I took my father's arm and stood next to him behind the closed doors. On the other side of the doors the organ music began to crescendo and the doors swung open. My eyes immediately fixated on the man waiting for me at the end of the isle. The look on his face gave wings to my heart. Joy, love, and contentment. This was God's plan for my life, the one he designed for me long ago, before I was born, and mixed in the center was this man I was about to marry. I couldn't wait to start our journey as man and wife. My heart was so full as God poured out his joy on my life. That day couldn't have been any better. I was content in the water of life I was sailing that day. It was a smooth sailing day.

As we embark on our life's journeys, we will encounter different types of waters. There will be smooth sailing and stormy weather and there will even be a time when we find ourselves dry docked or sitting in still waters.

Not every type of water is as harrowing as the high seas where you are clinging to your anchor for dear life as it's dropped, when you are "white knuckling" it on your knees. There are some waters where we can have our anchor held in place close by and enjoy basking in Christ's love. These are times when joy can be seen all around us, and we are content in our journey.

Have you ever had those times when you are outside, and everything is perfect? It's warm (not hot or humid), a gentle breeze is kissing your cheek, the sky is blue, birds are singing, there is green everywhere and colorful flowers, beautiful life in abundance in every direction. For a moment you stand there, close your eyes, take in a deep breath, and you smile. In that moment all is right in your life. Your heart is tranquil, you feel life is sufficient with everything you need, and so contentment is all you feel. This is smooth sailing: feeling all is right in

Lisa C. Whitaker

your life and joy abounds; you are content. The term "content" ("arkeo" in Greek) here, means "to be sufficient, to be possessed of sufficient strength to be strong, to be enough for a thing." [10]

Think of those times when you felt sheer and total joy. Those times when you were so happy, and you felt like you had the world by the tail. I'm talking about an overflow of energy, a "my cup runneth over" thing, a product of being lavished on. The day I got married was one of them for me. This kind of joy is something we cannot create on our own, it is what God gives us and it is nurtured by the anticipation of what God will do next in our life. In other words, if this part of life is this awesome, I can't wait to see what God brings next! This anticipation comes when we remember what God has done for us in the past that caused joy to develop in our hearts. It's recognizing the history we have in our relationship with God.

The days our first two kids were born were other "smooth sailing" days where I just basked in God's love (The birth of my twins was not so smooth if you remember). Now, obviously these days held some physical pain that hurt like all get out, but oh, how soon we forget that part as the nurse places that little baby on your chest. As I held each of these tiny lives in my arms, I could see so clearly the love of God. Each of these little ones held the hope of a future that excited me beyond measure. I allowed myself to stay in those moments for as long as possible soaking up the love as we sailed along.

One thing I must make clear here. When I talk about "dropping anchor" I don't mean that you keep this anchor in some closet and only pull it out when rough seas hit your life and you feel you need it. When you accept Christ in your life, your anchor is always with you. But sometimes we need to cling to it with everything in us and sometimes we just know it's there. Like those big Navy ships when they are sailing along, their anchor is secured on board in key places ready at a moment's notice to drop. Our anchor is also carried with us in key places: it is rooted deeply in our heart and mind. Always at the ready to be dropped and secured in the unshakable love of Christ Jesus. Perhaps the right thing to say is that when we accept Christ as our Savior, our anchor is already dropped and secured in his love at all times, but there are times when we need to "hold fast" to the lines of that anchor, to really grip hard or really cling to that hope we have in Jesus who is our anchor.

When you are in the smooth sailing waters know there is a warning that comes with the territory. When the water before us looks smooth like glass, and where joy abounds, we may be tempted to sail it by our self instead of depending on God. Now we enter a different kind of "content." Here, the Greek word is "autarkes" which means "sufficient in oneself, self-sufficient, needing no assistance." [11] Often when joy begins to wane; we will try to recapture that deep joy on our own by trying to get rid of the things in our life that hurt us. We keep people at arm's length, never enjoying a deep relationship. We look to substances that will "lighten our mood" or make us not "feel" those hurtful situations. We avoid taking risks; avoid stepping out in faith for fear of being hurt. That's what was happening to me before my marriage started failing and before my twins came. I had begun to try to create joy and contentment (the *arkeo* kind) in my life as my skies darkened and the waves began to build. I had been lulled into a stupor of contentment in my smooth sailing that I had failed to see my need for God. That is the main problem with the smooth waters in life, they mask the need for God. When you are living a life of self-sufficiency you don't notice the dark clouds that may be heading your way. Before you know it, those difficult times are right on top of you and you are suddenly jolted into attentiveness of a need for God. Psalm 62:8 says we should "trust in God at all times," and "pour out your hearts to him, for God is our refuge." The key words here are "At all times." Don't ever let there be a day when you are caught off guard by a sudden storm surge without having your anchor ready.

In the very beginning of time, Adam and Eve were content in their life. They had everything they needed, they didn't want for anything and there was beauty all around them. Genesis 3:8 tells us "the Lord God was walking in the cool of the day," so I'm thinking of those temperatures being perfect with the blue sky and lush greenery everywhere. Contentment was the perfect word for Adam and Eve's life until Satan showed up on the scene and questioned Eve's contentment. Satan made Eve think about how she could really be happy and content if she was not allowed to eat from one of the fruit trees. He encouraged Eve to shift her focus from all God had provided for her and Adam to the one thing he withheld from them. Eve made the mistake of not going to God with her questions first before accepting Satan's viewpoint. As Eve sailed along in her smooth waters, she failed to see her need for God. She, in the moment Satan questioned her, had become complacent with her life, feeling dissatisfaction with what she had as Satan pointed it out. In the blink of an eye, in a moment of misguidedness, she and Adam lost all touch with the true contentment they once had through God's provision and support.

Therefore, it's so important not to ever neglect such an incredible source of strength within you, your anchor (your hope in the finished work of Jesus on the cross). The enemy will always be looking to knock you off course, to capsize your ship and drown you.

It is imperative that you keep your anchor in good working order. Check it daily for rust. Keep the working parts oiled so it will be ready to function smoothly when you call on it. How do you keep your anchor in good working order? By remembering daily, the things God has done in your life. By rejoicing in all God provides for you and shows you. By communicating with God daily about the things on your heart and mind. By daily reading and studying scriptures, it is his navigational guide for our lives. Include Christ in every aspect of your life. When you do this, you allow Christ to connect with you in life, and the end result will be a victory in the big storms that is so much more joyful than you could possibly imagine.

Be thankful for the smooth, quiet days when nothing major is happening. Instead of being bored with the quietness or routineness of life, use this time to seek God's face. What do I mean by this, you ask? To seek God's face means to make an effort to get to know him more personally. It means to converse with him through prayer and worship him. It means to search out his character and quiet yourself to listen for his voice. Seeking God's face is getting to know him, not bombarding him with requests, making your time together all about you. God wants us to seek to spend time with him in his presence more than anything else. As we do this, God promises that we will find him (Jeremiah 29:13). God's word instructs us to seek his face in Psalm 105:4, "Look to the Lord and his strength; seek his face always." Why is this important? Because seeking God's face means we are seeking his presence. You can learn a lot about a person when you meet with them face to face, when you can look into their eyes and actively listen to what they are saying. Psalm 63:1-3 paints a beautiful picture of what it means to seek God's face, "O God, you are my God, earnestly I seek you; my soul thirsts for you, my body longs for you, in a dry and weary land where there is no water. I have seen you in the sanctuary and beheld your power and your glory. Because your love is better than life, my lips will glorify you." Does your body long to find God? Is that not a great visual of how desperately we should desire to seek God's face?

As you travel the smooth sailing waters seeking to meet and find God, he will transform routine and quietness into joy. David wrote in Psalm 131, "God, I'm not trying to rule the roost, I don't want to be king of the mountain. I haven't meddled where I have no business or fantasized grandiose plans. I've kept my feet on the ground, I've cultivated a quiet heart. Like a baby content in its mother's arms, my soul is a baby content. Wait, Israel, for God. Wait with hope. Hope now; hope always!" (The Message). This humility David exhibited shows us how to be content with God's leading in our lives. The picture David paints of the baby in the mother's arms is a great visual of contentment being near the one who can satisfy our desires. The baby is not crying and screaming, he's just content to be held.

This is a great picture for us to have when we are sailing in smooth waters. We can, in our humility, be content being close to Jesus, the one who can satisfy our desires, the one who can hold us in every circumstance, the one who can produce true joy in our hearts. Paul tells us in Philippians 4:10-13 the secret to being content in all circumstances is drawing on Christ's power for strength. We can only do this when we are walking close to him. When you begin to walk closely with Jesus you will notice that you will start seeing things from his perspective. As you sail along with Jesus close to you, your priorities will begin to shift to what he deems important, not what you want or think you should do. As you begin to yield to God's priorities for your life, contentment in the journey comes. So, in short, the way to find true contentment in life lies in your source of power, your perspective, and your priorities.

In John 14:16-17, God says he gives us a helper to be with us forever. The Spirit of Truth that will reside within us, and who will go with us through every water of life we experience. If we listen to him, he will guide our paths and he will sound the alarm bells when we begin to deviate off course.

Those big Navy ships go through daily

inspections and routine maintenance whenever they are out to sea. The anchors are checked during these times to make sure they remain in good working order. The Navy sailors are confident that when they need to drop them, they will work most effectively. How confident are you about your anchor? Is it a bit rusty or have missing links? Is it crumbling or is it shiny and strong, ready for anything?

God tells us in Psalm 32:8, "I will instruct you and teach you in the way you should go; I will counsel you and watch over you" (ESV). By starting your day in communication with your Creator, you will find you will be equipped to handle whatever comes your way. Before you set sail full speed ahead, do your inspections. Then as you go out, keep your anchor close and at the ready. By lingering in God's presence, you will be able to stay on the right heading and will be prepared to change course when he says turn.

As much as I would have loved to stay there in my "smooth sailing" days of marital bliss, I could not, and you shouldn't expect to remain in a smooth sailing day either. Eventually, the first marital argument came. The exhaustion of sleepless nights and crying babies darkened my blue skies. Feelings of inadequacy and unworthiness became a recurring issue in my life. Blue skies turn to grey and the winds begin to howl.

PHILIPPIANS 4:11-13 (MSG)

"I've learned by now to be quite content whatever
my circumstances. I'm just as happy with little as
with much, with much as with little. I've found the
recipe for being happy whether full or hungry,
hands full or hands empty. whatever I have,
wherever I am, I can make it through anything in
the One who makes me who I am."

CHAPTER 6

DRY DOCKED

The year 2000 was a dry-docking period for me, the USS Lisa Whitaker. In the few years leading up to this one, my husband had suffered through Guillain-Barre Syndrome. A year later he took a new job and we moved to a place where we knew no one and family was far away. My marriage hit a brick wall and I became pregnant with the twins, something I was sure God had mistakenly given me instead of my sister who had always wanted multiples. The twins came via emergency C-Section and seven weeks premature. As I've already mentioned, I spent many days visiting the Neonatal Intensive Care Unit praying these babies would survive. The breaking point finally came when we almost lost Aaron, one of the twins, at two months of age.

What happens when you experience several highly stressful events in a relatively short period of time? The answer is a change in your body's chemistry that can lead to depression. Let me tell you, I had not only entered the barrel of depression, I had just about hit rock bottom of the barrel. I felt no love, no desire to be around people, especially my family. I felt nothing. I was basically numb to life. It's as if my body just shut down; my engine turned off. My thoughts circled at times around the idea of suicide. Though I was in this state of mental trauma, I still cried out to God. I still conversed with him daily, usually through tears. Sometimes the words I had for God were not good ones, but still, I was connecting to him.

I was very good at putting on a mask when I had to be out around people, pretending like I was all "put together" in life. Most people outside my immediate family had no idea the turmoil my life was in; they never saw the emptiness I felt as I moved around in our home. For all intents and purposes, I was in the middle of the desert just waiting for my life to end. There was no apparent spiritual growth, no joy, and no reason to get up in the mornings until one day an opportunity arose to go on a trip with my sister and mother to Scotland and London. When my sister asked if I would like to go, I jumped at the chance thinking that perhaps if I just got away, I would be able to get myself back to "normal." I kept my mask on while on the trip and to the best of my ability I acted like I was having fun. I "oohed and ahhed" as we toured the various tourist attractions, and I smiled for pictures in front of each castle and monument, but my heart felt cold. I normally would have been so geeked out traveling about a different country that displayed a wealth of history, but all I could think about was how dead I felt in my life.

The trip began to wind down and eventually I was faced with going home. The morning we were due to fly home I cried a lot! Oh, I made up stories about how much fun I had and how I didn't want it to end, but I think my Mom started to suspect something when the crying wouldn't stop. Once our flight arrived in Atlanta from London, my sister, mother, and I had to say good-by and part ways since they were flying on to Indianapolis and I was flying on to Chicago. When I arrived at my gate, I learned my flight had been cancelled and the announcement said to see a gate agent for rebooking. I checked the board to see if my sister and Mom's flight was still on time and it was, so I didn't even contact them to let them know mine was cancelled.

My first thought was that I have a ticket I could change to go anywhere and just disappear. I sat for a long time holding that ticket trying to figure out where I would go. In the back of my mind, as I was contemplating this, were the precious voices of my children. What would happen to them if I just left? I could actually hear them crying out for me, not understanding where I had gone and why I had left them. I was beginning to feel pulled in different directions. The tug to disappear was very strong and was twisting my heart. In a voice so clear that it quieted the chaos in my mind, God spoke to me and down-right commanded me to go home. With tears in my eyes, I approached the gate agent and rescheduled my flight for Chicago. I was going home. God had used the voices of my children to reach my heart. He was in the center of this spiritual war zone for my life and he was fighting hard for me.

Can I just say how amazing it is when God fights for you? In Deuteronomy 20:3-4 God tells us he will go into battle with us and he will fight for us. Listen to what he says, "And he (God) shall say to them, 'Hear, O Israel: Today you are on the verge of battle with your enemies. Do not let your heart faint, do not be afraid, and do not tremble or be terrified because of them; for the Lord your God is he who goes with you, to fight for you against your enemies, to save you' (NKJV). I could so easily hear these words with my name inserted. "Hear O Lisa: Today you are on the verge of battle with your enemies. . ." What precious Scripture to remember when the battles rage in life!

Nothing changed over the next few weeks after returning home. The trip to Scotland had only made me not want to be at home even more. At home one morning, I sat on the floor of our bathroom with the door closed, my head between my knees and tears softly cascading down my face. Without a knock or an invitation to enter, my husband opened the door, came in and closed the door behind him. He looked straight into my eyes and said, "You are not leaving here until you tell me what is wrong!" I gently shook my head and simply responded, "I don't know what is wrong. I just don't feel anything anymore." With that response, my husband was adamant that I go see my doctor. I made the appointment and to make sure I followed through in going, my husband went with me. The diagnosis: Full blown depression. According to my doctor my body chemistry was so wacked out that it was no wonder why my mind was all over the place. Her solution was to put me on medication for a year to see if she could get my body back to a balanced state. It did only take a year to get me straightened out with the help of that medication, but my lifeline in all of this was my anchor that I have always had with me. It was dropped and secured in God's love and I was holding fast to it. Even at my lowest point I stayed connected with God. My anchor was secure and holding strong even though I felt weak. Remember, when I had gone through that ordeal when Aaron almost died at two months of age; God had grown my faith exponentially knowing I would need it to weather this time of maintenance work.

I had once completed a Bible study on the Book of James and on one of the days the author wrote: "Everyone thinks they would rather have sunshine than showers. But what would the earth look like if it never rained again?" [12] I pondered this question and the short answer is that it would look dead. It would be a desolate and barren desert. There would be no productive growth because there would be no flow of water to nourish it. This described my life exactly during my time of depression.

Are you wondering how this story connects to being dry-docked? Let me explain. When the storm clouds darken our skies, we yearn for sunshine and joy, but God knows we need both sunshine and rain to grow us and make us into the person he wants us to be. When God thinks we are ready for another growth spurt, he may say "not yet" to our pleading to stop the downpour of our suffering. God will lead us into a place where he can do a little maintenance work in our lives so we can eventually shine with his blessing. Just like that Bible study author said, all that sunshine would make a desert and that's how it is in life. Without our trials and difficulties our lives would be completely void of beauty, character and depth, therefore God may need to shut our engines down temporarily to make some changes. We have to remind ourselves when this dry-docked period comes it will be temporary and will be well worth it in the end. We must trust God's sovereign control to do what is necessary in our lives to make us better equipped to persevere through this life between the "already" and "what is yet to come."

I liken these "dry-docked" times to pruning or clearing away the dead leaves. When your garden has limbs or flowers that are not growing or have become dead-looking, you take your pruning shears and you cut them off. In the fall, you cut many of your plants back ahead of time to prepare it for a more fruitful bloom in the spring. Dry-docked waters are when God gets his pruning shears out and begins to shape you and get you ready for a bigger "bloom" in your faith. I will not sugar coat this! It hurts! It's often a struggle and I didn't like it one bit! Yes, my faith in Jesus was stronger coming out of the ordeal with our son, Aaron. I had learned the hard lesson that God was in control and I was not, but I still had areas in my life that were not growing. I still had a tendency to "go it alone" and not ask God for help first. I still held on to pride, thinking I was strong enough on my own to navigate some of the waters of life. I held on to pride when I thought more of what others would think of me than what God would think of me. I needed some serious pruning and this time of depression stripped me of this pride issue.

When my husband and I left the doctor's office after getting my diagnosis, I threatened him with my leaving him if he ever told anyone about the diagnosis. This diagnosis was a full-on blow to my prideful self. I did not want anyone to know that I was not able to cope with life at that particular time in life. I wanted to keep my "I have my life all put together" persona at the forefront, but out came the pruning shears. A few short years after my diagnosis and getting through the year of medication, I was asked to speak at our women's bible study. Now I had prepared well, having done my research, reading, study, etc. I was ready. When that morning came, something didn't feel right. God kept telling me "Lisa, I want you to tell the women about your depression." My response was "Umm yeah right, God, I don't think so!" He began to press harder as I drove to the church. My hands began to sweat, and my heart rate picked up. "I really don't want to do this Lord, please don't have me do this!" I mean we went back and forth on this until I was standing at the podium and I had gotten through most of my talk and then it came. I paused in my talk and I looked up and out at all the faces staring back at me and I knew this was the time to tell my story. My mouth opened and with every word I spoke, I felt God snipping away the prideful leaves that had prevented me from blooming. My life, at that point, was laid bare before these women. At the foot of the stage laid a pile of brittle, stunted, and dead areas of my life that were ready to be discarded. Luckily, my depression story fit right into the lesson for that day. When God directs your actions, the impact is much greater.

The feedback from the women afterwards was amazing. So many had suffered the same diagnosis. So many had felt ashamed that they too had to be put on medicine for it. Out of my period of "dry-dock" (or pruning) came my first blossom. As these women opened up and shared with me their struggles with depression, I felt my faith, my trust, my love for God get stronger. The "engine" of my life was running again, and I knew God was sending the "USS Lisa Whitaker" back out to open water. God had allowed all these previous life situations to prepare me and to move me into this dry-docking period. Nothing was wasted. Each prior situation produced in me what was needed to sustain me during this. Romans 8:28 says, "And we know that in ALL (caps are mine) things God works for the good of those who love him, who have been called according to his purpose." And Romans 5:3 tells us, ". . . we also rejoice in our sufferings, because we know that suffering produces perseverance; perseverance, character; and character, hope."

You will not experience the "desert" or "dry-docked" place only once in your lifetime. Know that there may be several times when you find yourself there. This desert is a place where your life feels so dry, a place where you feel nothing is growing, and you find no pleasure or beauty. Dry-docked is a time in your life when you feel you can't move forward; you are stuck in the chaos of your life and you get to a point where you begin to shut down. The key to your ignition is turned off. These are times when your anchor needs to be dropped and firmly secured in God's love for a long period of time: dry-docked. Even though there are sufferings (desert places) all around us, we can find joy in the saving grace of Jesus Christ through faith. We must trust God is working in our lives during this time and when his maintenance work is done, we will be able to set sail again.

Think of those big Navy ships again. There are times when these ships must be brought back into port due to maintenance work. When things get broken on the ship it will need to be docked in order for a crew to fix what is broken. It cannot sail out onto the blue waters until this is complete.

Sometimes, this docking period lasts longer than what we would want, but it will, in God's eyes, be a short time. The key here is that when you have faith, hope, and trust in the finished work of Jesus Christ (your anchor), it will secure you firmly and hold you in place while you are struggling to have fixed what is broken in your life. It will tether you to God's stronghold while the maintenance work in your life is being conducted.

It is during these dry-docked times that God is doing a work in your life to mature your faith. There are faith lessons to be learned. There are exercises of strengthening your faith being performed. There is pruning being done. Jesus told us in John 15:1-2, "I am the true vine, and my Father is the gardener. He cuts off every branch in me that bears no fruit, while every branch that does bear fruit, he prunes so that it will be even more fruitful." He goes on to tell us in verse 5 that we must remain in him in order to bear this fruit and that apart from him we can do nothing.

Once completed, your engine's ignition will be turned on and revved up and you will be able to secure your anchor on board and sail out under blue skies and calm waters once again. You will be stronger and have a renewed confidence in the direction God has pointed you. Once again you will see joy and the beauty that surrounds your life as you sail, but never far from view is the anchor that stands at the ready at the forefront of your heart.

John 15:1-2 (NIV)

"I am the true vine, and my Father is the gardener.
He cuts off every branch in me that bears no fruit,
while every branch that does bear fruit he prunes.

CHAPTER 7

HIGH SEAS

Across the table from me, our son, Aaron, chatted away about the times he had posted that morning at the big swim meet he was competing in with his team from University of Michigan. It was lunchtime and the coaches gave him permission to have lunch with his dad and me before heading back to his hotel to get rested for the finals session that evening. Always believing he could do better, he talked easily of the changes he thought he could make to get faster, to make his stroke more efficient. The clamoring of dishes and the voices of the others that occupied tables in the restaurant faded in the background as I watched and listen to Aaron process his thoughts. In my pocket my phone vibrated, alerting me to an incoming text message. As I began to read the message, my heart stopped, and a lump formed in my throat. The message was from a friend of mine telling me that our son's very dear friend from high school was killed in a training accident at Fort Hood. He was a cadet at the U.S.

Military Academy.

My eyes drifted slowly upward looking at our son and wondering how I would tell him this news? My heart was breaking not only for this young man's family, but also for what my young son was about to endure. Aaron looked up and locked eyes with mine and for a brief second there were no words spoken. As he saw the tears building in my eyes he quietly asked, "What's wrong mom?" My husband had also stopped eating and both were intensely looking at me waiting for me to speak. I could hardly get the words out, the vocal cords strained from the lump that found its home there. As my words began to sink in, Aaron's heart began to crumble. There in the midst of the noisy restaurant I witnessed my son experience, for the first time, the death of someone close. First the tears came, then the sobs. My husband quickly moved to the other side of the table and enveloped our son into his strong and loving arms. Nothing could be said, we could only love at that point. As we sat with our son back in our hotel room, I prayed for this cadet's family. I imagined what it must have been like to get that knock on the door only to open it to find the uniformed military officers standing there with grief-stricken faces ready to give you the worst possible news. I thought of this family and how their world has come crashing down around them, how the storm and high seas of life have come out of nowhere to rock their world. My mind drifted to our own son who was also on his training exercise that summer with the Naval Academy. He would have to be told of this tragedy too, but we would not be able to be with him when the news hit. Prayer would be our only arms of love. Since this heartbreaking moment unfolded, my Bible has remained opened to Psalm 91 as I pray for our son's safety and the safety of his Naval brothers.

Think of the worst thing you have endured so far in your life. At the time it seemed as though you could not bear it; would not make it through. Yet, here you are. You may not ever want to endure that again and perhaps you won't, but you will have other hard times of a different kind. God promises that he will always be with you when you pass through the waters. He says in Isaiah 43:2-3, "When you pass through the waters, I will be with you; and when you pass through the rivers, they will not sweep over you. When you walk through the fire, you will not be burned; the flames will not set you ablaze. For I am the Lord, your God, the Holy One of Israel, your Savior." Passing through waters of difficulty will do one of two things. It will either cause you to drown or force you to grow stronger. Trying to navigate these waters in your own strength will likely result in you drowning. But if you take God along with you, he will protect you and see you through.

What is it about the high seas of life that affects us so much? It is the "fear" element that it can cause. It's the sudden fear of being alone in the situation, it's the fear of the unknown, it's the fear of not surviving, it's the fear of change. However, if you have Jesus Christ in your life, you can be sure that whatever situation he has allowed to come into your life, he is right there with you through it all. We do not have a Deliverer or Savior who sits far off and doesn't "do life" with us. Our Lord lives with us and lavishly loves on us. His protection can always be counted on (Psalm 46:1 & 5). God's Word is full of verses that tell us God is our strength in times of trouble. Two of my favorites are Psalm 37:39 and my all-time favorite, Psalm 46:1 – "God is our refuge and strength, a very present help in trouble" (NKJ).

God promises that if we have accepted Christ as our Savior then nothing can separate us from his loving presence (Romans 8:38-39). This is the basis of our security. Whenever we start feeling like our life is spiraling out of control or that the waves are so high we might not survive; we need to remind ourselves our security rests in God alone because he alone is totally trustworthy. He alone is powerful enough to save. We will never be in control of our life circumstances, but we can trust and secure ourselves in his control. He tells us in Psalm 46:10 we just have to be still and know that he is God.

The important thing here is to not just have this

"head" knowledge, but to actually trust it. Trust it like you trust that chair to hold you as you sit down. When the storm clouds roll in, you should have no doubt as to where your anchor will fall or what stronghold it is secured in. When I am faced with a storm, I like to close my eyes and imagine my anchor aboard the USS Lisa Whitaker, being released and those two sharp hook points grabbing firmly into the solid surface, the foundation beneath me. My faith and trust in the person of Jesus Christ is being asked to hold me firmly in his perfect love for me. Can you see it? Can you see yourself holding fast to that anchor rope like the early sailors did during a storm? If you believe God is your strength in times of trouble, then you will stand confidently knowing your anchor will be secure and you can weather anything life throws at you. Psalm 56:3-4 says, "When I am afraid, I will trust in you. In God, whose word I praise, in God I trust; I will not be afraid. What can mortal man do to me?" This is not always an easy thing to do though. Lee Strobel writes in his book, *A Case for Hope* that "it's often easier to count on God to redeem our past than it is to trust him with our present and our future. [13] How easy it is to start relying on our own self when the waves begin to build even though we have our anchor at the ready. Paul addresses this problem with the Galatians when he wrote "Are you so foolish? After beginning with the Spirit, are you now trying to attain your goal by human effort?" When the waves begin to build, do you immediately begin to figure a way out of danger, or do you immediately go to God in prayer and ask for help?

Have you ever contemplated how nice it would be to not have that paralyzing fear during troubled times? To be able to have such confidence that God is in control, which means we don't have to be? That everything will work together for the good because you have chosen to trust and believe in Christ Jesus? (Romans 8:28). Having that kind of confidence will change your whole perspective on the circumstances you find yourself in. Instead of heart pounding, mind trapping, emotional ambush, you will find peace in the midst of the storm. This is what God has been reminding me of and teaching me as I have been struggling with life as a military mom. Which would you prefer to experience? If you are a follower of Jesus, then you can draw on the fact that God gives us the power to conquer. Romans 8:37 says, "No, in all these things we are more than conquerors through him who loved us." You see, we don't have to fear life or death, or whatever storm is happening now in your life or even the ones that will come in the future because Jesus loves us and he gives us the victory.

Remember the story I told you of our son, Aaron, when he was born? For a time, I had chosen the heart pounding, mind trapping, emotional ambush route. Believe me, it was a horrible road to go down, but once I fell to my knees and gave it all over to God's control the peace came. I don't mean the heartache was not there anymore, but that this calmness, this feeling that no matter what happens going forward, I would survive and be okay. I could let go of my desperation to control my situation and just let God do what was in his will to do. It's funny to think back and know Jesus was with me the whole time. He was trying to give me his perfect peace, but I was too busy fighting him for control. How stupid was I? I was trying to go it alone; I was trying to figure a way out myself instead of going directly to God.

I think back before this time in my life, and I always said I was a believer; that I had faith in Christ. However, when I finally came through to the other side of this whole ordeal with Aaron as an infant, I realized I really didn't know what it truly meant to be someone who followed after Christ. I believed what I read about Jesus, but did I really have a secure belief "in" Jesus? Was my faith really "in" him? Was I confident "*in*" his power? I'm not so sure it was.

Faith is to trust. Not only to believe, because as I mentioned earlier, "for even the devil believes the truth that there is one God and trembles" (James 2:19 NKV). Faith isn't something you get to avoid troubles. That is almost like putting your faith in faith itself and that will not be a secure anchor that saves. Faith is something you develop and grow in in order to endure troubles. In this faith, it's all about the relationship you have with Christ. You develop the relationship and you grow in it; you begin to trust *in* who he is not just about who he is. Faith is to believe and to trust what our human eyes cannot see. Belief *of* Jesus is NOT the same as belief *in* Jesus.

I think of the story in the Bible (Matthew 8:23-27, Mark 4:35-41, Luke 8:22-25) when the disciples were in the boat with Jesus and the storm came. They were terrified and thought they were doomed. Why were they afraid? Did they not remember all the amazing miracles they witnessed Jesus perform? Did they not remember how Jesus restored life to the widow's dead son (Luke 7:11-17)? They were afraid because the raging storm was about to crush them, and their faith was not *in* Jesus' power over the forces of nature. They had put their faith in the boat to protect them and so the storm was able to unleash gripping and paralyzing fear in their hearts.

Let me just interject here that a ship cannot be sunk by the water that surrounds it unless that water gets inside. When we accept Christ as our Savior, he keeps us sailing upright and our vessel airtight when the seas of life crash around us. His protection keeps the harmful evils from getting inside and trying to separate us from himself. The disciples were letting the water get inside their boat. They had their eyes on the storm around them, which opened the gateway for fear to creep in and begin to sink their ship. Letting go of the storms of this world and seeing them as no threat is what it means to believe *in* Jesus, to believe *in* his power. Only when you trust the Father and *in* Jesus can you let go of the fear that grips your heart and master whatever storms are surrounding you.

When you read what Jesus said in the Scriptures, listen for what he tells you *not* to put your faith in. "Will wealth save you from death? No! Will food save you from suffering? No! Can you find security from a husband/wife? No! Can a boat save you from sinking in a storm? No! Nothing on earth will offer you salvation from the storms of the here and now or the ones to come. At some point you have to realize there is only one person who can offer the kind of deliverance you want. His name is Jesus. You must let go of the things you hold so tightly to in this world and cling to the Savior, our anchor, in order to master these devastating storms.

In Lee Strobel's book, *The Case for Faith*, he said, "When your world is rocked, you don't want philosophy or theology as much as you want the reality of Christ." [14] You can have all the religious head knowledge in the world, but when you come face to face with the most dire of circumstances in your life all you want is for Jesus to be who he said he is and for him to keep his promises made to you as a believer.

We are to be ready to come face to face with situations totally beyond our ability to handle on our own. Jesus says, "be anxious for nothing." In Greek the word anxiousness *means to divide the mind.* When we talk of having a divided mind during an impossibly difficult storm in life, the division refers to security versus fear. So, here is the big thing to remember. Drill this into your head! You cannot expect to be fully resting in God's ability to save and be full of fear at the same time! They do not go hand in hand! If we want to be free of the fear that keeps us from fully resting in God's saving ability, we must let go of everything else we believe will save us. You cannot even rely on your vast knowledge of earthly things to keep fear from controlling your heart, because it is only our faith in Christ's power that secures and saves. You and I must decide which of these, fear or security, will control our minds.

So when these storms arise in our lives we drop our anchor in God's love (our complete faith in the finished work of Jesus Christ on the cross) and by doing this, we are dwelling in the shelter of the Most High and thus we are able to find rest in his shadow (Psalm 91:1).

If your security rests squarely in Jesus Christ, then whatever storm raging in your life at this moment should not be able to throw you into the darkness of fear. Whether God chooses to deliver you from this storm or not, your soul is safe with him. This is the ultimate deliverance. All that is in this world is temporary, but what Jesus offers and has in store for his followers is eternal. That is a true and unshakable hope for us. It is the solid surface our anchor digs in to and holds to. There is an old hymn by Edward Mote called "*My Hope Is Built on Nothing Less.*" In the second verse he writes, "When darkness veils his lovely face, I rest on his unchanging grace; In every high and stormy gale, my anchor holds within the veil." [15] I love this! When those massive storms come and they are so dark that you can't see God's face in it, his grace is still present, it has not departed from you and if you cling to that, your anchor will hold.

The Cadet's family I spoke about is in the middle of the worst storm they will probably ever face on earth. There is not a more dire time than now to have their anchor secured in God's love. I pray with all my heart that they truly do have their anchor secured for if they do, they can rest in the hope that one day they will hold their son again in their arms for an eternity. This is exactly why Jesus willingly endured the cross so that we could have that eternity with him to look forward to. With this hope as our anchor, we can safely say to our loved ones who also have a faith grounded in Jesus, not "good-bye," but "see you soon." As I sat with our son during this cadet's funeral, I listened as different people talked of this young man's character and his love for life and others. They talked of love and loss and how Jesus comforts us through it all. The gymnasium was packed with family, friends, government officials, and other cadets who were in his graduating class at the Military Academy. I prayed that the hearts of each one would be touched by the words from Scriptures that were read, and this young man's family would be drawn close to Jesus. Our son received a bracelet that day that had this young cadet's name inscribed on it and the date he died. It also had the American flag and the Academy's emblem, which read "Steel Hearts." It has been 3 years since his death and our son still wears the bracelet as a reminder of their friendship, the loss he has felt, and the hope he has that one day they will see each other again. I love the idea of having a "steel heart." Not in the sense of having a heart that is cold and heartless, but rather a steel heart in the sense of it being strong, unshakable, and sure, in my Savior, my anchor.

You can have a strong and confident heart when it comes to your faith in Jesus. But having your anchor secured in God's love does not mean your heart will not still be shredded or that you won't feel the deepest pain you have ever felt. But God's love means he is right there with you in it; he is grieving with you, comforting you in it. He promises that though there is sorrow now, joy will come with the morning (Psalm 30:5). This doesn't mean the very next day you will be joyful, it means there will come a time when your heart begins to heal and it will be able to feel joy again. There will come a time when the storm ceases and you find yourself standing and your heart begins to beat again. There will come a time when the story of your life God has just given you will be required to be retold to someone else going through a similar situation and your story will bring comfort to them.

George Muller once said, "Be assured, if you walk with Him and look to Him, and expect help from Him, He will never fail you." [16]

First John 5:4-5 says, "For everyone who has been born of God overcomes the world. And this is the victory that has overcome the world – our faith. Who is it that overcomes the world except the one who believes that Jesus is the Son of God" (ESV)? In this passage John tells us whoever knows and believes in God's Son, and believes he is the Christ, has been born of God and has eternal life (there is the family line idea again). This is that hope the top part of our anchor symbolizes; it is connected to our faith and trust, which makes it complete.

There is a passage in one of Charles Spurgeon's sermons that I love. It said, "Christian, remember the goodness of God in the frost of adversity. Rest assured that when God is pleased to send out the biting winds of affliction He is in them, and He is always love—as much love in sorrow as when He breathes upon you the soft south wind of joy." [17] When those storm clouds build and race in, look to God. Know that he is in your storm and he brings with him his love to anchor you. Remember what he did for you through his own Son, Jesus on the cross and through his resurrection. This is the anchor that saves! *HOLD FAST* to it!

1 JOHN 5:4-5 (NIV)

"For everyone who has been born of God overcomes the world. And this is the victory that has overcome the world – our faith. Who is it that overcomes the world except the one who believes that Jesus is the Son of God.

CHAPTER 8

STILL WATERS

Have you ever had a time in your life when you felt stagnant, sitting still and just waiting? Like you were not moving forward (or backward)? Perhaps you have been praying for something but it seems like God is silent and so you find yourself waiting for clarity.

Let me ask you a few more questions. When you pray for God to do some work in your life, how long do you keep praying for this? If you don't get your answer in the next twenty-four hours do you stop praying for it? How about if you don't get an answer in the next five years? When God doesn't move in your life when you think he should, do you take matters in your own hands and try to answer the prayer yourself? Do you get tired of waiting on God?

Someday you may find yourself just sitting in the water with no strong current driving you in the direction you want to go or what feels like no wind in your sails to move you forward. You're praying for God to show you which direction to go; to move you, but the wind doesn't come and so you sit.

What does it mean when God is silent? Am I

asking too many questions? Ask yourself a question then. "What is God trying to teach me?" Remember, God has a plan for your life! He doesn't make up this plan as he goes along. It was determined from before you were even born (Psalm 139:16; Jeremiah 29:11). In accomplishing his plan for you, many things must move and work to be completed. This all takes time, and this is not on our timetable but God's! In the waiting process there are usually lessons that need to be learned, either by you or someone involved in God's plan for you, before the plan can move forward.

What is important to remember is that while you wait, Satan will begin to whisper lies into your ear. He will get you to wonder if God even knows or cares about you or wonder if God is even out there. Be prepared for that! Waiting feels long in the duration of the trial, and the wait can be the hardest aspect. Proverbs 13:12 declares, "Hope deferred makes the heart sick." This means when your hopes or expectations don't pan out the way you thought they would, when you thought they would, you become frustrated, discouraged or maybe even depressed. You may begin to doubt. You begin to doubt God's goodness, his power, or even his existence. That doubt becomes unbelief when we give up hope in God.

There is a sweet little passage in Scripture that talks about how all of creation, even those of us who believe in Christ, groan as we wait with eager anticipation for our future glory. Groaning is a low, guttural sound that originates deep within. It is a sound that has no words, but its sorrowful, painful meaning is understood. It is much like the sound someone in agony will make. Have you experienced this kind of groaning in your wait for future events? It's amazing to me to think that even the world is groaning in its wait to be transformed; to be once again in a perfect state in which God created it to be. We groan because we have experienced the goodness of the Spirit while waiting here in this life and now, we are eager to have that which is promised in paradise. We groan because in the here and now, we suffer from all kinds of trouble instead of having what we are promised, what we are waiting for in paradise. This scripture in Romans 8 tells us this future glory is what we hope for and it's because of this hope that we were saved. It says "hope that is seen is no hope at all. Who hopes for what he already has? But if we hope for what we do not yet have, we wait for it patiently" (Romans 8:18-25). How is your patience in waiting going? Are you groaning? If you are, tucked within these Scriptures in Romans 8 is some encouragement for your waiting. In verse twenty-six we find out that when the waiting gets hard, when we don't even know what to pray for anymore, "the Spirit, himself, intercedes for us with groans that words cannot express." Wow!! The Spirit groans for us. I cannot fathom what that looks like. But I love what it feels like in knowing he is so passionate about us that he steps in with inexpressible words and takes our need to the throne room of God.

A few years ago, I did a study on Joseph. Now there is a guy familiar with the idea of waiting. Time after time he was put through the ringer and yet he faithfully waited for God to deliver him. As you read through the narrative, it seemed as though

Joseph couldn't catch a break, and we find ourselves wondering if we could have been so patient. But there was Joseph, still bending the knee to God and waiting. He was thrown into a pit and then sold into slavery by his own brothers, but he waited on God. He was sold again to Potiphar in Egypt, one of Pharaoh's officials, the captain of the guard, but he waited on God. Just when Joseph thought God was moving in his life, he was accused of trying to rape Potiphar's wife and was thrown in jail. Again, he waited on God. Joseph had to wait on Pharaoh's cup bearer to remember him in jail, a two-year wait, and by the time God brought Joseph's family to Egypt, Joseph had waited on God for about twenty-two years before a reconciliation with his family occurred.

As I read through the story of Joseph, I often wondered why God would let such terrible things happen to Joseph? Why didn't he protect Joseph from them? If God is in control, why was Joseph suffering so much? Reading through the account of his life, it seemed as if God wasn't present for Joseph. However, there are two little words that change everything in Joseph's world: "*but God.*" Many times, in the story of Joseph Scripture says God was with Joseph. Even though Joseph experienced many trials, he kept God at the center of it all and, in the end, we see the outcome. Many things had to be worked out in Joseph's life and many people had to move before the final blessing could be accomplished. Genesis 45:5-8 tells us it was not Joseph's brothers who sent Joseph to Egypt, but it was God. Joseph's brothers' actions were meant for evil against Joseph, *but* God meant them for good. If God had not allowed Joseph to go through these hard times, many lives would have been lost (including his own family) due to the severe famine in the land. God had to work through his plan to get Joseph into a position of power within the Egyptian kingdom in order to save his people, Joseph's family, from starvation. You can read through Joseph's story in Genesis 37-45. It's a good one!

During the hard times in our lives, God still occupies the throne and he is working. It is called "providence." Providence is the protective care of God. It means that since God knows the future, he will make provisions ahead of time to protect or work his plan. He puts things in place in a timely manner for future events. These preparations God is working out takes time and as hard as it is, we must be patient and wait. Romans 8:14 tells us "But if we hope for what we do not yet have, we wait for it patiently." That word "patient" is not one of my favorites! Waiting is hard enough but to do it patiently is like nails on a chalkboard to me. When God tells me to wait patiently, I respond with "I may look like I'm being patient on the outside but on the inside, I am scratching my eyes out!"

Sometimes we have to wait because Satan has put roadblocks in the way. In Daniel 10:12-21, we are told God sent an angel to instruct Daniel, but the angel was waylaid in a battle against the "prince of Persia" or one of Satan's demons. This angel had to battle this evil spirit until the archangel Michael showed up to defeat him. This passage continues to show us that when one demon is defeated, another takes its place (prince of Greece: vs 20). Evil is an ongoing battle. Even now, though we may not see it, a battle is being fought between the angel armies of God and those who belong to Satan. I find it comforting, knowing all of God's angels are ministering spirits that he sends forth to help all of those who have placed their faith in Christ and will inherit salvation (Hebrews 1:14).

God promises he will take all the horrible times in our life and for those who believe in him he will work them for good (Romans 8:28). We can claim this promise and have confidence that as we are enduring a trial, God is going to work it for some good in our life just as he did for Joseph. Remember it is impossible for God to lie (Hebrews 6:18). What he promises, he will do!

If the waiting you are doing right now deals with a physical need, know that healing isn't always immediate. There is no guarantee we would get a physical healing this side of heaven, but God declares to us that our heart condition is more important than a physical healing.

At the age of twenty-one, I was diagnosed with Crohn's Disease and it was horrible! I was engaged to be married and the plans that my soon-to-be husband and I had were not turning out like we had planned. By the time we had our first baby, the disease had gotten worse. I never ventured outside our home unless I knew if there was a bathroom available at the place I was going. I can even remember times when our daughter was crying in her crib and I couldn't get to her because I was on the bathroom floor curled up in a ball and engulfed in pain, unable to move. For years I would be placed in and out of hospitals, I'd be put on this drug or that drug and nothing seemed to work. I was one of those people who began to fall prey to Satan's whispers; I wondered if God was even listening or if he really cared. I waited for about thirteen years before God said, "the time is now." After being admitted once again to the hospital in extreme pain, my doctor believed my Crohn's was blowing up again, but I knew different. Something inside of me just felt different and I kept telling the doctor this. Despite my convictions, a colonoscopy was ordered, and I was put into a twilight state for the duration of the procedure. Right before being taken to the surgical room, one of our pastors came to pray with me. He prayed to Jesus, our great Physician. He prayed for a healing that would deliberately awaken my hope in him once again. I quietly promised God that if he would heal me from this Crohn's Disease, I would tell everyone I could about what he had done in my life. I was desperate so yes, I tried to bargain with God. I was not totally dense enough to think I could entice God with my offer, he doesn't need me to accomplish his work, but I was hoping he would see my desperation and have compassion. When the procedure was over and the doctor came to my room with his report, what came from his mouth, at first, seemed like a dream. I asked him to repeat himself. His words were, in short, "If I were seeing you for the first time today, I would never have diagnosed you with Crohn's. There is nothing there, you are clean." Oh, and the pain I was having that landed me in the hospital in the first place was completely gone. It was as if this was God's way of giving me a concrete confirmation that he had heard me all those years I had been crying out to him and when the time was right, he acted. I am clean!! I have been in remission for about twenty-five years. Thank you, Jesus. In case you are wondering, yes, I tell the story of my healing whenever he opens a door for me to tell it.

In all these trials, God writes a story for our lives and these stories are meant to be told to others he places in our path. God had heard my prayers, but he also heard my promise and within a year or two after this healing happened, I was asked if I would share my story in a book being published called *Treasure In Jars Of Clay*. There was not one second of hesitation on my part. God often uses our stories to encourage others who are struggling in the same way we did or may even bring another person to a place where they place their faith in Jesus for the first time. These are huge blessings!

As I began writing this book, I hit another waiting period where God just wouldn't send the wind for my sails. My direction, the ideas and words weren't coming; I couldn't write for a long time. I would re-read what I had already written hoping it would direct me in what to write next, but nothing came. It was like this for almost a year. During this year, many things happened in my life. My daughter got married, our son graduated from the US Naval Academy, our two other sons also graduated from their universities and God pushed me to write and deliver two lectures back to back to a lady's bible study at our church. In all these events came trials and struggles for me, and more lessons to be learned and more writing material to go with them. But I had to wait until God worked through them all with me. Some of these struggles are currently ongoing but I know God is in the middle of them. I look forward to the day when he accomplishes his plan for each of them!

I love what King David said in Psalm 27:13-14. He said, "I am still confident of this: I will see the goodness of the Lord in the land of the living. Wait for the Lord; be strong and take heart and wait for the Lord." David, in all the trials he endured, was confident that in his present life God would see him through it all. David is another person who was very familiar with waiting. He was anointed King at the age of sixteen but didn't become king until the age of thirty. That's a long wait! During this wait time, he was chased all over kingdom come and threatened repeatedly by the current King, Saul, who was jealous of him. Where was God in all of that? Well, he was working. He was teaching David to trust him, to rely solely on him as his deliverer. When you find yourself waiting on God, make good use of this time by searching out what God has for you to learn. Quiet yourself before him and ask him to show you what you need to learn and then listen for him to respond.

Let me tell you about one of these times of strife in my life during this waiting period that resulted in an overflow of blessing. I have done lectures before, but I had not done two of them back to back until now. When I felt God asking me to do this, my first response was "umm I don't think so God." Preparing these lectures takes a lot of time and research and study so doing two of them at the same time seemed a bit overwhelming given everything else that was going on in my life at the time. In true God-fashion though, he would not let that be my answer, so he kept pushing. He can be so bossy sometimes.

As I began to read and study and research, I began to see the path God wanted me to follow with these two lectures and it was obvious they were connected. It would be a kind of a two-part lecture on how God writes your story through rough times. After I finished writing the first one, I thought it was the reason God wanted me to do them both. I knew it would be a blessing for those who heard it and would entice them to attend the second lecture. He was so faithful in giving me direction! However, the day I finished the rough draft of the second one (literally four days before I was to give it), I was exhausted and not even sure it made sense. I decided to take a break and go for a run on some trails near our house. When I arrived at the park, I ran into an old friend that I hadn't seen in a while. In our conversation, he began to tell me how he was struggling with a very big family hurt. He told me he was so mad at God and that he was not even talking to him anymore. As I listened, I suddenly started recalling everything I had just written in my last lecture and even from the one before. Instead of spouting off right then and there though, I felt God telling me to just be quiet and listen. After my friend and I parted ways, I continued on my run listening to God prepare in my head what he was going to have me put down on paper, in letter form, to send to my friend. When I returned home, I immediately sat down and wrote every word God instructed me to write and I mailed it. A few days later I got a text message from my friend expressing his sincere gratitude for the letter. He was so touched by the words (God's words not mine) and they made such an impact not only on him but also his wife who also read it. Every point made in this letter God had had me make in the two lectures I had prepared.

If the encouragement my friends received through the words God had given in these two lectures was all that was meant to be, I would have been ecstatic. There is no greater feeling than knowing God has used you to minister to another hurting soul, but God was not done. After I had given the second lecture, I had many women come up to tell me how much they could identify with different parts of it. One, in particular, was a widow in our church whose husband, a minister at my church, had passed away several years prior. During that time of high seas in my life when our son Aaron almost died as an infant, this pastor was the one who placed the card on the back of Aaron's little hospital bed that read "be still and know that I am God" (Psalm 46:10 NKJ). In this lecture, I told this story of struggle in my life and how this pastor, not knowing the impact that card would have in my struggle, listened to the leading of God and placed that particular card there as he prayed for little Aaron.

Now I had not known this widow would be in the audience that day, *but* God did. She came to me after the lecture with tears in her eyes and told me how touched she was to hear of the faithfulness of her husband. It brought so much joy to her to know of times when his obedience to God made an impact in the life of someone else. This sweet widow then told me they too had lost a child early on in their marriage. Not only did her husband understand what I was going through at that time, but now she was sharing her story with me. We were able to encourage one another in a common heart for what God does in the lives of those who love him.

Talk about being blessed. My cup was overflowing with God's love and blessings for my obedience in writing and delivering these two lectures. For the entire time of preparing these lectures, I struggled with feelings of being overwhelmed, exhaustion, feelings of inadequacy, and the list goes on. *BUT GOD!* All that chaos came together in such an amazing way. A story was written in my life that he used to impact others and here I am getting to tell you this story now, in this book, because God had me wait until the timing was right, until he could bring me through this with a clear vision of his leading so I could then return to the writing of this book.

You see it's important to remember God is relational. Everything he does is to deepen the relationship he has with us. Beth Moore said in her book *Get Out of That Pit*, "Even the faith in God that an intense wait demands is about relationship. God calls upon us to walk in faith because faith requires a partner to place it in." [18] I love this! I couldn't think of a better partner to place my faith in than God, the one who will move heaven and earth to be able to walk with me as he did with Adam and Eve in the garden.

Psalm 130 is such an encouraging piece of Scripture! It speaks to the "waiting" and the promise of what comes when we wait. It says, "Out of the depths I have cried to you, O Lord; Lord hear my voice! Let your ears be attentive to the voice of my supplications. If you, Lord, should mark iniquities, O Lord, who could stand? But there is forgiveness with you, that you may be feared. I wait for the Lord, my soul waits, and in His word I do hope. My soul waits for the Lord more than those who watch for the morning – yes, more than those who watch for the morning. O Israel, hope in the Lord; for with the Lord there is mercy, and with Him is abundant redemption. And He shall redeem Israel from all his iniquities" (NKJV).

When we wait for God, he promises many good things: redemption (abundant), renewed strength (Isaiah 40:31), blessings beyond belief (the Bible is full of these examples and I've already given you some of mine). Some people will wait only a short time, others may have to wait years. Look at Abraham and Sarah (Genesis 18:1-15 & Genesis 21:1-7). They had to wait until they were in their 90s to have their first baby and that baby was the beginning of the promised lineage of our Savior Jesus Christ. God's chosen people had to wait forty years to enter the Promised Land because of a plethora of disobedience that needed to be dealt with first. Those were long times to wait! Could you have waited that long for an answered prayer or for direction from God? It's hard! Even Abraham and Sarah tried to "help" God complete his promise of an heir. What a disaster that turned out to be. God's chosen people, time and again, got tired of waiting for God and tried to make their own god to follow (Exodus 32:1-35). Again, a very big disaster!

When we get impatient waiting on God and try to do things our own way, unfortunate consequences usually follow. However, if we endure the waiting, the blessing that comes will knock your socks off!

Our daughter, Talor, was 29 years old when she married her husband Adam. During her high school and college years, she had a few dates with nice young men, but Talor knew each one wasn't right for her. She waited and waited for God to bring her the right guy. She did fall hard for one young man and at the time he seemed like he might be "the one," but when she wouldn't break the purity commitment she had made to God with this guy, he bailed. Since she was a little girl, I had always prayed for her future husband. I kept telling her to be patient, that God was preparing him for her and there were things in her that he had to prepare for him too. I think there was a time when she didn't think God's plan for her included a husband, but I just kept praying and telling her to pray and be patient.

Then one day, out of the blue, came Adam Bassett. He walked into her life and God rewarded her for her faithfulness in waiting. Their relationship had God at the center from the start. When planning their wedding, they honored God by making it more about their relationship with him rather than just a wedding. I watch them together and just chuckle at how God has blessed them abundantly with joy and laughter. Things would have been much different if she had settled and given in to her desire for a husband. The waiting was hard and there were many tears along the way, *but God!* Oh, those two little words mean everything. They are the game changers! Will you choose this day to wait on God whatever the circumstance?

Sometimes our waiting will endure until we see eternity. When tragedy enters your life and you are left asking "why," you may have to wait until you see Jesus face to face to get the answer. The promise he makes that we need to remember during these times is "In all things God works for the good of those who love him, who have been called according to his purpose" (Romans 8:28). This promise doesn't say it's only "some" things, it says "all" things. That means that the loss you just suffered, the job you just lost, the relationship that was torn apart, whatever it is, God will work it for your good. He will use that situation or circumstance in your life to further his kingdom and bring glory to himself, but you may have to wait.

We may have to wait for a time for deliverance or answers to our "why" questions, but we never have to wait on God himself. We never have to wait to experience his love or his presence in our lives. The only wait then is on seeing his work displayed in our lifetime, seeing our prayers come to fruition (unless he chooses to have you wait until you reach eternity to see it).

You know, each day gives us an opportunity to make a choice to sit in our chair of hope, to put it on like we put on our clothes or we can choose to wallow in our hurt and blame everyone and especially God for it. Remember the story of Joseph we just talked about? If anyone had ample opportunities to wallow it was Joseph. Life seemed to go wrong for him at every turn, but he chose to wait on God. He chose every day, to sit in his chair of faith that God is working all things for his good. He chose hope! In the end, we see what God had worked out. Joseph ended up in a position to save a people and especially his family from a severe famine (Genesis 37:1 – 50:26).

Waiting on God doesn't mean we just sit around and wait for God to do something. Waiting on God requires action on our part. We don't just wait – we wait in hope. The Wiley Online Library defines our biblical hope as "a confident expectation of what God has promised and its strength is in his faithfulness." [19] So, we wait, believing and trusting God will complete what he set out to do, what he has promised to do. We live with confidence and courage in God's presence and promises. We wait with our anchor secured in the hope he gives us.

Was Joseph always comfortable in his wait? Absolutely not! Did he ever endure pain while waiting on God? Indeed, he did! Was I comfortable in my wait for healing? No! Was my daughter having a blast in her waiting for a husband? No! God's grace often comes to us in uncomfortable forms. The working of his plan often includes things we would not have chosen for ourselves. We have to remember that when those difficult times come and we are waiting for God, those moments are not an interruption or a failure of his plan but that they are part of his plan. We must remember the words, "*But God.*" It is God working to complete what he has begun in your life. Keep your anchor secure in the hope Christ has given you! Guard your mind against the whispers of Satan. The wait will soon be over and whatever God brings to fruition will have been worth the wait.

Psalm 27:13-14 (NIV)

"I am still confident of this: I will see the goodness of the Lord in the land of the living. Wait for the Lord; be strong and take heart and wait for the Lord."

PART III

COMPASS DUE NORTH

CHAPTER 9

LOOKING TO THE HORIZON

When our daughter, Talor, graduated high school, the motto she chose to put on her invitations said, "You will never discover new lands unless you have the courage to lose sight of the shore" – Andre Gide.

God doesn't want us to stay tied to the shore, to be tethered to the dock. He never meant for us to be stationary or never putting ourselves out there. He wants us to live and live fully in him. You will never know his full blessing in your life unless you have the courage to set sail. As you set sail, making sure your anchor is at the ready, you will begin to discover the many amazing things God has planned for your life. With your anchor active and in position, you can go out in confidence that God has set out with you and will never abandon you when the waves begin to build.

You should never say, "If I just trust the Lord, I will never experience hardship." Trust me, hardships will come! There will still be pain, but the question is, will you choose to still trust him in the pain? Habakkuk 3:18 says, "Yet I will rejoice in the Lord; I will take joy in the God of my salvation" (NKJV). Living and rejoicing in those things that cause pain requires a choice made by you alone. You either say, "yes" to continuing to rejoice in the Lord or you say "no" in which case you still have made a choice. Take the joy of your salvation with you as you set sail. This is your firm foundation that gives a secure place to drop your anchor during the rough times. When you have this joy of salvation with you, you should never feel the need to play it safe in life. With your hand gripped tightly in the hand of Christ you will be able to walk each day in confidence.

I have a paper pinned to the wall next to my desk with Psalm 112:7-8 written out on it. It reads, "He [the upright man] will have no fear of bad news; his heart is steadfast, trusting in the Lord. His heart is secure, he will have no fear; in the end he will look in triumph on his foes." This is the joy of my salvation! It is looking adversity in the face and knowing, without a doubt, that God still occupies the throne in heaven. Do you want to know what it looks like to be anchored in Christ's love – the hope he gives through the gift of salvation?

Look at 2 Corinthians 4:7-10, 16-18. "But we have this treasure in jars of clay, to show that the surpassing power belongs to God and not to us. We are afflicted in every way, but not crushed; perplexed, but not driven to despair; persecuted, but not forsaken; struck down, but not destroyed; always carrying in the body the death of Jesus. . . .So, we do not lose heart. Though our outer self is wasting away, our inner self is being renewed day by day. For this light momentary affliction is preparing for us an eternal weight of glory beyond all comparison, as we look not to the things that are seen but to the things that are unseen. For the things that are seen are transient, but the things that are unseen are eternal" (ESV). The treasure spoken of in verse seven is the message of salvation through Christ. This message has been entrusted to us, a frail and imperfect people, by God, thus the jars of clay image.

With your eyes fixed on the horizon, trust in God's plan for your life. He tells us "For I know the plans I have for you, plans for good and not for evil, to give you a future and a hope" (Jeremiah 29:11 ESV). Make sure your anchor is secure in the love God has for you, a love that drove him to sacrifice his Son for you. Know the joy that comes with the assurance that Jesus will help you to navigate the waters of life so you will arrive at your eternal destination safely. Paul David Tripp said in his *New Morning Mercies Devotional*, "The entire hope of fallen humanity rests on this one thing – that there is a Savior who is eternally steadfast in redeeming, forgiving, reconciling, transforming, and delivering love." Tripp also says "He knows, he understands, he is in control of what appears to be chaos, he is never surprised, he is never confused, he never worries or loses a night's sleep, he never walks off the job to take a rest, he never gets so busy with one thing that he neglects another, and he never plays favorites." [20] One more thing you need to remember here. No matter what kind of water of life you are traveling through, God is always with you; he is traveling through it with you.

Remember the story of the disciples I told you about earlier? They were in the boat when this big storm blew in and they feared they would be crushed beneath the waves, but did you notice who was in the boat with them? Jesus! The water is crashing over the sides of the boat and the disciples are holding fast to whatever they could get their hands on, but right there in their midst was their Savior. In fact, Jesus led them out into the water knowing full well they would encounter this storm. What did Jesus say to them when they woke him from his slumber (and by the way, who can sleep when being pelted by rain? Jesus can!) "You of little faith, why are you so afraid?" Never once did they think "hey, we will be just fine in this storm because Jesus is with us." Nope, their faith was in the boat. Just as it was with the disciples, Jesus sails with us. He is in our boat in every part of the journey we are on, in every kind of water we encounter. Jesus promises us in Matthew 28:20 that he "will be with us always, even unto the end of the age." Knowing he is with you in every water of life, do you cling to him or to your boat?

Have you ever looked at a beautiful tapestry? Like really looked at it? Turned it over even and looked at the backside? When you do, you will see the beauty is only one-sided. It is the finished product that we see from the outside that is beautiful. However, if you turn it around, it is all chaos. You can't really see the picture for it is all distorted. This is our life here on earth. It may be all "chaos" looking to us now because we are not able to see the whole finished picture, but God sees it complete. When Jesus went out on the water with the disciples, he already knew the storm would come and he already knew what the disciple's response would be. Our God is a God who sees, not just in part, but he sees the whole. That's why it is so important to trust him with the decisions of our life, to let him guide you toward the horizon. Let him be the captain of your vessel. Not seeking God's guidance in the decisions of your life would be like trying to sail your ship without a compass.

Ephesians 2:10 says, "For we are God's workmanship, created in Christ Jesus to do good works, which God prepared in advance for us to do." Some translations use the word "masterpiece" to describe what we are to God. I giggle at the thought that I could be a masterpiece of any kind, to anyone! In Greek the meaning for workmanship can be interpreted as "fabric" or "art." Each one of us is a thread in this fabric and each thread is being woven together by God, to create this beautiful masterpiece (or work of art). Can you see yourself as a work of art, a masterpiece? With every pull of the thread God makes in our life, he is completing a little more of his big story. As we set sail with our vessel's compass pointing to the True North (Jesus), we will encounter opportunities to serve Christ out of the love he has filled us with. These acts of service will weave together the lives that are touched by these acts, and yet again, complete a little more of the masterpiece God is creating (keep thinking of that tapestry).

Keep in mind some of these acts of service that connect to other lives may come from enduring some of the storms of life. God uses these times to refine us and make us stronger so we can help others. First Peter 1:3-9 talks about how we may have to suffer in grief for a little while in all kinds of trials but that these have come so our faith may be proved genuine and may result in praise, glory and honor when Jesus Christ is revealed. When gold is heated, all the impurities float to the top and can be skimmed off. Steel is tempered or strengthened by heating it in fire. Likewise, our trials, struggles, and persecutions refine and strengthen our faith, making us useful to God. The ultimate masterpiece God is weaving together will not be completed until Jesus returns to put the final "knot" on this world tapestry.

Scriptures have always pointed to Christ even thousands of years before he came to earth. The prophets foretold his coming. He has remained the focal point or the True North of this life here on earth. The internal compass for each one of us has always been pointing to him. However, not all of us have consulted this compass or even acknowledged it. Some of us have chosen to veer off course in search of our own earthly treasures or to create our own tapestry of life. The thing about "earthly treasures" is that they don't last. In Ecclesiastes 3:11 we are told "God has also set eternity in the hearts of men . . ." God programed our hearts to desire our eternal home in heaven, our treasure, so the pursuits of earthly treasures will not satisfy us. So many people spend a lifetime searching for the treasures that satisfy them here on earth, not realizing only our treasure in heaven is truly satisfying. Our hope in this treasure is what allows us to have that sense of contentment while on earth as we wait for it.

Scriptures say (in Matthew 6:19-21) that moths and rust destroy earthly treasures and thieves break in and steal them. (Have you ever seen what moths can do to a tapestry that's not properly cared for?) I can attest to this last part as recently we had a thief who decided to smash the window of our son's car as he stopped in Atlanta for dinner on his way to his next assignment with the Marine Corps at Fort Gordon in Georgia. The thief (or thieves) stole a laptop, and other personal things along with his Marine Corps sword that was issued to him upon graduation from the Naval Academy. Some of the items taken not only were valuable (by this earth's standards) but they had sentimental value as well. This individual or individuals were only seeking their own desires or treasures. We were hurt, saddened and angry that these things were taken but they, in the end, are just "things." They will have no bearing on our eternal treasure chest. This thief will have to answer for his actions one day and so I have had to leave it at that. What is most important is to keep my compass pointed in the right direction.

Jesus tells us point blank "where your treasure is, there your heart will be also" (Matthew 6:21 ESV). This thief's heart is obviously tethered to these "earthly treasures." When Christ puts that "final knot" on this earth and all these earthly things are burned up, what will this thief have left? Jesus says, "no one can serve two masters. Either he will hate the one and love the other, or he will be devoted to the one and despise the other. You cannot serve both God and money" (Matthew 6:24).

On the horizon is our final destination and

when I reach it, I personally want to hear Christ say to me, "well done Lisa, my good and faithful servant." I want to have confidence that when that final knot is placed, I will have a treasure waiting for me in heaven, my true home. How about you? What treasures are you storing up as you journey toward the horizon? Where is your heart? What master are you serving? Is your compass pointing in the right direction? With a compass pointing toward the horizon and our final destination of heaven, we will be able to step out in confidence each day knowing Jesus is with us. He is the Master we are serving. Whatever we encounter along the way, we know there is a treasure waiting for us at the end.

2 Corinthians 4:7-10; 16-17

"But we have this treasure . . . to show that this all-surpassing power is from God and not from us. We are pressed on every side, but not crushed; perplexed, but not in despair; persecuted, but not abandoned; struck down, but not destroyed. We always carry around in our body the death of Jesus, so that the life of Jesus may be revealed in our body. . .Therefore, we do not lose heart . . . . For our light and momentary Troubles are achieving for us an eternal glory that far outweighs them all."

CHAPTER 10

FINAL DESTINATION

You and I are traveling right now between two different realities. The "what has been" and the "what is yet to come." What you do in this "in-between" matters a great deal because one day we will pull into port and drop our anchor for the last time in eternity. We will finally be home. Home will look very different to each of us depending on the decisions we make in the "now" or the "in-between" time. If you have already placed your faith in the person and work of Jesus Christ, your course for home is already set to what Jesus calls Paradise (Luke 23:43). The compass of your vessel is already pointing in the direction of home. If you have not yet made that decision to follow Christ, you are currently on course for a home that is a far cry from paradise. The good news is that it is not too late for you to change course, to get your compass pointing in the right direction.

Listen to what Jesus tells us, what his promise

is to us, "Do not let your hearts be troubled. Trust in God; trust also in me. In my Father's house are many rooms; if it were not so, I would have told you. I am going there to prepare a place for you. And if I go and prepare a place for you, I will come back and take you to be with me that you also may be where I am. You know the way to the place where I am going" (John 14:1-4). If you choose to trust God's promises, then a room is being prepared for you. Jesus says you know the way because your internal compass has been set on a course for that home. Then just to make sure you fully understand the way, Jesus says, "I am the way and the truth and the life. No one comes to the Father except through me" (John 14:6). He is telling us to make sure our compass is pointed toward him, the True North, and when the time comes, we will pull into the safe harbor and drop anchor for the last time. Home!

I have often thought about the room being prepared for me. Is it just a simple room with a neutral color pallet or is there wallpaper in my favorite colors? Are there beautifully woven rugs to warm my feet and a lamp by my bed so I can read my favorite books? Or will my room be large and filled with finely woven tapestries and beautiful paintings depicting God's creation? Will there be crystal chandeliers and gold trim along the ceilings and walls?

As a junior in college at Ball State University, I

had the incredible opportunity to study abroad with BSU's London Centre Program. During my time in England I visited a variety of castles and palaces such as Windsor Castle, Warwick Castle, Blenheim Palace, and Longleat House as well as many others. Walking through each one I was struck by the lavish décor that overwhelmed my eyes. The large beautiful paintings so rich in color, the carvings in the wood trim along the walls and staircases, the tapestries that were so beautifully woven they almost look like paintings. Every room had crystal this and crystal that, gold this and gold that. There were marble fireplaces and marble statues, and in the bedrooms were large canopy beds all with delicate wood carving details. I couldn't imagine living in such extravagant surroundings, but Scripture paints for us a picture of heaven that will rival even that of the richest of castles here on earth.

The book of Revelation, the last book of the Bible, gives a beautiful description of what home will be like – paradise or heaven. Chapter 21 of Revelation describes a picture of a place where there will be no more death, mourning, crying, or pain. It talks of the brilliance of heaven (from God's glory) that shines like a very precious jewel, like a jasper, clear as crystal. There are twelve gates made of pearl with twelve angels at each gate. It has twelve foundations each decorated with every kind of precious stones. Jasper, sapphire, chalcedony, emerald, sardonyx, carnelian, chrysolite, beryl, topaz, jacinth and amethyst all set in place in those foundations. The streets of the city are made of pure gold, like transparent glass. The glory of God will be its light and the Lamb its lamp, no need for a sun or moon as there will be no night there. (I'm thinking I won't need a lamp to read by.) Nothing impure will ever enter it. Keep reading the Scripture passage in Revelation 21 and 22 for more detail! When you finish reading about heaven, know this one thing. Whatever picture you have formulated in your mind about heaven, it will be exponentially more beautiful. Our minds cannot even begin to conjure up its awesomeness! I believe there will be so much grandeur to explore that it will take an eternity to do it. First Corinthians 1:9 says, "No eye has seen, no ear has heard, no mind has conceived what God has prepared for those who love him." We can read all the Scripture that describes for us what it will be like, but our minds are so finite that we won't even come close to imagining its beauty.

Now to be fair, if I am going to share with you what the home in heaven will be like, I should also give you a glimpse of what the "other" home will be like for those who choose not to drop their anchor in God's love, those who choose not to place their faith in the saving grace of Christ. In several places in the Bible Jesus uses the words darkness, weeping, and gnashing of teeth to describe what hell will be like.

Now just think about this for a moment. Many people have the idea hell will be one big party with one big bonfire in the middle and they will be with their friends living it up for eternity. This is not what Jesus is depicting at all. First darkness. Second Peter 2:17 calls it the "blackest darkness" reserved for those who decide to follow the sinful nature, those that just live life for themselves. Because God will not be present in this "home" it will be utterly dark. Have you ever been in a place where there was absolutely no light and in fact you could hold up your hand in front of your face and couldn't see it? It's kind of creepy right? That is the atmosphere of hell. Because God's glory will not be present, there will be no light. Because God's love will not be present, there will be no source of comfort, love, or peace, only constant weeping and pain. Because God's hand of protection will not be present, there will only be suffering and evil, the gnashing of teeth. Second Thessalonians 1:8-9 tells of this separation of God's presence when it says, "He will punish those who do not know God and do not obey the gospel of our Lord Jesus. They will be punished with everlasting destruction and shut out from the presence of the Lord and from the majesty of his power." Destruction here doesn't mean annihilation or non-existence; it means loss or ruin for eternity. It means you will not be destroyed to the point where you will not exist anymore, it means you will exist for an eternity feeling the effects of loss and ruin forever. Revelation 14:11 indicates that there is no rest day or night for those who choose this home. In other words what you will feel and experience 24/7 for eternity is utter darkness, pain, both physical and mental, suffering because that pain will never cease, evil at every turn, weeping for what you know you could have had with Christ. Forever and always! (For more detail on these descriptions read the following verses: Matt. 8:12, 13:42 & 50, 22:13, 24:51, 25:30, Luke 13:28). It is a very sobering thought to say the least! Again, if you have not yet chosen to follow Christ as your Savior, your True North, you are on a collision course with this eternal port and that is where the anchor you have chosen to cling to will be dropped for the last time.

Several years ago, I was privileged to be able to go on a trip with my sister and some friends to the South Pacific islands of Tahiti. We flew to the island of Papeete where we then boarded the M/S Paul Gauguin. At the time we began to leave port and set sail, it was nighttime. As the ship rumbled to life and began to pull away from land, all the lights on the ship went out and as we stood on the deck of the ship it suddenly became very dark. They do this so that the many lights that illuminate the ship don't inhibit the captain's visual ability to steer the ship out of the port safely. As we looked out to sea, there were no lights and no separation of sky and water.

It was completely and utterly dark. I put my hand in front of my face and I could not even see it. That was a disturbing moment to say the least! I could hear those around me talking and laughing but I couldn't see them at all. It was a feeling of being completely alone and yet not alone. When we were a safe distance from the harbor, the lights came on and our journey began. This period of darkness seemed like a very long time, but in actuality it was only a few minutes. Hardly an eternity, but it gave me a small glimpse into what the atmosphere of a life without God's presence would be (minus the laughing). For that brief time, I became uneasy, a little unsettled. Can you imagine how it would feel to have that as the atmosphere for an eternity? I just got shivers down my spine thinking about it.

During my time sailing around the Polynesian Islands, I bore witness to such beauty that I can't do justice putting it into words. I do remember one morning sitting on the deck of the ship with my sister and looking out at the Island of Bora Bora as we ate breakfast. We were anchored just offshore so we had a beautiful view of the island. As I sat there looking at the majesty of the volcanic mountain covered in lush greenery and the beautifully designed bungalows that reached out into the water and all of it set against the most incredible crystal blue waters I have ever seen, I thought "this has to be a sliver of what paradise will be like." I could not take my eyes off the picture before me. I humbly thanked God for sharing with me this amazing creation of his, for giving me the wisdom to know that this creation was his doing and that what he has prepared for me in the "not yet" will be infinitely more beautiful. I cannot wait! As much as I enjoyed my time on this trip, it was the coming home at the end of the trip that held the most joy. Being reunited with family and friends after being away for a long period of time was the best. There was energy, excitement, and strong, deep hugs from my kids who said, "we missed you more than you know!" (And we are overjoyed that we will not have to eat pizza one more day after having it six out of the ten days you were gone). There was the warm embrace and tender kisses from my husband that let me know he too had missed me beyond measure (mostly because he had been the sole caretaker of our four kids for ten days). That feeling of coming home held everything from love to familiarity to comfort to joy to peace and finally a rest that is easy. This is what it will be like when you arrive and drop anchor for the last time at your final destination (only a bazillion times better) if you have chosen paradise as your eternal destination.

What is it you will hook your heart and soul to today in the hope you will receive life eternal in paradise? What anchor will you use to give you courage, hope, and the ability to put one foot in front of the other in a world of chaos that is in the middle of the "what has been" and the "what is yet to come?"

Can I just put in here that if you have given your life to Christ and you know where your eternal home will be, then you should know that when you get there you will glorify God and enjoy him forever. However, you don't have to wait until you arrive at that final port before you can enjoy what is available to you at your final destination. You can start now by blessing God through your praise and worship for who he is and what he has done for you through all the waters you have traveled so far. When you do this, you will find that he will lavish his blessings and goodness on you in the here and now – his perfect joy! When you think about all the blessings you will receive at your final destination, it will influence all that you do along your journey to get there.

Anchor your heart and soul to the One who is faithful to save, and the One who loves you more than life itself, the One who has the power to calm the storms, Jesus Christ. In your life, your circumstances will continually change, your boat will rock but again, Jesus promises to always be with you. His promises provide your heart with the peace and contentment that can withstand any storm and when you talk to him; when you pray to him, he wants you to remind him of his promises. Not that he doesn't remember them, but because it gives glory to him. It brings joy to his heart to hear you say them.

Learn his promises, they are the true treasures you should be storing up here as you walk this earth. Jesus is the True North your compass should be pointed toward. You may not realize it but the path your life takes is directed by what you put your hope in. It truly does set the direction of your life. Our hope only functions as good as whatever we anchor it to. You may have placed your hope in some other person, or a dream you have or in some other belief system and this is what your life will be shaped by. This is what your course is set by. It's where your compass is pointed. Can you say your hope is anchored to something sure and firm? Are you confident in where your compass is pointing? Can you truly say you are looking forward to your final destination?

Hebrews 12:2-3 tells us to "fix our eyes on Jesus, the author and perfecter of our faith, who for the joy set before him endured the cross, scorning its shame, and sat down at the right hand of the throne of God. Consider him who endured such opposition from sinful men, so that you will not grow weary and lose heart."

Romans 5:1-5 tells us perfectly about the hope we can have in the love of Jesus. It says: "Therefore, since we have been justified through faith, we have peace with God through our Lord Jesus Christ, through whom we have gained access by faith into this grace in which we now stand. And we rejoice in the hope of the glory of God. Not only so, but we also rejoice in our sufferings, because we know that suffering produces perseverance; perseverance, character; and character, hope. And hope does not disappoint us, because God has poured out his love into our hearts by the Holy Spirit, whom he has given us." We have been justified or made right through our faith – we have a new family line in which we now live, remember? In this new family line, we have peace, we have rejoicing, we have hope that doesn't disappoint, and we have the Holy Spirit as our guarantee of the family we now belong to. These are what shape our lives because it is what we are anchored to.

Remember in chapter two when I said God confirms his plans through multiples? Well, let me tell you about the big Kahuna of them all. In I John 5:6-8, 11, God confirms that his son, Jesus, "came by water and blood and that it is the Spirit that testifies, because the Spirit is truth." This is the same Spirit God has given to us. He says, "For there are three that testify: the Spirit, the water, and the blood; and the three are in agreement." Now for what they are in agreement about, verse 11 says "And this is the testimony: God has given us eternal life, and this life is in his Son." God confirms this and he cannot lie!

The Spirit cannot lie (he is truth)! Jesus cannot lie because he is God! If this doesn't cause you to rejoice in the hope of the glory of God, I don't know what will. Because of God's confirmation, you don't have to hope you have eternal life, you can "know" you have it!

If you have never tried dropping your anchor in Christ's love and all the other places you have tried to secure yourself to have failed to hold, why not try his love? Why not "taste and see that the Lord is good" that you will be so blessed when you take refuge in him (Psalm 34:8)? What have you got to lose? Allow me to put this question to you in a different way. What would you lose if you put your faith in Christ and all of this turns out to be not true? Answer: "nothing really." You will have lived a life that is good and filled with hope. However, what would you lose if you don't place your faith in Christ and all of this does turn out to be true? Answer: "your soul", "an eternal home in paradise," "an eternity in the presence of Jesus and all he encompasses." That's a lot to place at stake, isn't it? Jesus is praying to God the Father in John 17 and he says in verse three, "Now this is eternal life: that they may know you, the only true God, and Jesus Christ, whom you have sent." To stake your life on an eternity in paradise, you need to establish a relationship with God the Father and the One whom he sent, Jesus. Is it worth it? You must answer that for yourself, but from my perspective, absolutely!

"Whether you have realized it or not, Jesus is what your heart has been searching for, because what you've really been searching for is what God has created in you to desire. When he knit you together, he created you to desire life. The kind of life that is heart-changing, and heart-satisfying. What God has created in you to desire is to live life to the fullest, and abundantly. This true lasting hope of life that we desire is never found in the things or people of this earth. It's only ever found in a relationship with our heavenly Father, his Son Jesus and the Holy Spirit.

It has taken me some time to come to terms with having a son serving in our country's military but what a couple of years of lessons I have learned in the process! As a parent, it's always hard to pry your fingers off your kids' choices for their future and when that future involves voluntarily being placed in harm's way it's even harder. *But God.* Oh, those sweet words. What I have learned is that The Great I Am inhabits all situations, relationships, and locations by his grace. He is in you. He is with you. He is for you. He is our hope. He is the only anchor that can and will secure your life for an eternity.

So here it is. God is extending to you his gift. He is telling you in Deuteronomy 11:26-28 that he is "setting before you today a blessing and a curse" ("life and death"). He is asking you to choose life, and to love the Lord your God, to listen to his voice and to hold fast to him, to not turn aside from him. The choice is yours and yours alone to make. If you have already made that decision to choose life then you have the assurance of being sealed for eternity, so just remember to stand firm and hold fast while you wait for it. If you have made the decision to choose life you have already changed family lines. You are now an heir of the King!

Our trials are always a dark place for us. They often come as a complete surprise and many times they throw us into complete despair. It is important to remember that God is never surprised or unsure about these times. Daniel 2:22 says, "he reveals deep and hidden things; he knows what is in the darkness, and the light dwells with him." In that dark place we may be enduring, we cannot see the outcome and that is what terrifies us, but nothing is hidden from God. He is that light in the dark; that beacon calling us home. He always knows the outcome; he already sees the completed tapestry or masterpiece.

If you really want to know the solid ground you are dropping your anchor in, how powerful our stronghold is for our anchor, read Isaiah 40:12-31. The New International Version Bible Commentary says this about these verses: "God is almighty and all-powerful; but even so, he cares for each of us personally. No person or thing can be compared to

God. We describe God as best we can with our limited knowledge and language, but we only limit our understanding of him and his power when we compare him to what we experience on earth." [21]

Isaiah begins these passages describing God's power to create. Listen to this, "Who has measured the waters in the hollow of his hand, or with the breadth of his hand marked off the heavens? Who has held the dust of the earth in a basket, or weighed the mountains on the scales and the hills in a balance?" This blows my mind! Turn your hand over and look at the hollow part of your palm. Now think about how big the oceans are, the lakes, the rivers are. I don't know about you, but the hollow of my hand is pretty small. Not one person, no matter how big their hands are could measure the vast waters. How about the dust? I know my house alone would have to have a fairly big basket for all the dust it houses. Scripture says God holds the dust in "a" basket, it's singular – one basket. For my allergy's sake, I'm glad I don't have to be around his one basket! I'm excited to know that in eternity, I won't have to deal with allergies. Don't forget about the mountains and the hills. Have you ever seen a mountain in person? Can you even begin to know how much a single mountain weighs, let alone multiple mountains? Do you know how to balance a hill? I didn't even think that important, but if God has done it then it must be important.

Isaiah follows God's power to create with his power to provide and sustain. Who else has the know-how to sustain what has been created? In these Scriptures Isaiah says that no one is smart enough to counsel, enlighten or teach God. No one and nothing can compare to God's power. From where God sits, we and everything of this earth below are nothing – a drop in a bucket to him. Verse 22 actually says "its people are like grasshoppers." He has the power to "reduce rulers of this world to nothing," all God has to do is "blow on them and they wither, and a whirlwind sweeps them away like chaff" (verse 24). God himself, in verse 25, asks each of us a very pointed question. He asks, "To whom will you compare me? Or who is my equal?" Isaiah says for us to "Lift your eyes and look to the heavens: Who created all these? He who brings out the starry host one by one and calls them each by name. Because of his great power and mighty strength, not one of them is missing" (verse 26). When I am facing a difficult circumstance and fear is trying to get the best of me, I go outside at night and look up at the stars and remember this verse. I think it impossible for us to count the number of stars in a night sky, but God knows each one of them. Not one has ever been lost. I only have four children and when they were young, I must admit I lost one or two of them a time or two.

Finally, Isaiah describes God's presence to help

us when we need him. Despite the fact that we, compared to God, are worthless, he never gets weary taking care of us. The journey we take in this life is often compared to a marathon instead of a sprint. I have never run a marathon, but I have trained for and run a couple of half-marathons. During the months of training prior to race day, I had good days, bad days and down-right horrible days. There were days when I thought I could not take one more step. There were days when I had to run into the wind and felt like I was being pushed back more than moving forward. There were days when I found myself running in the rain and feeling cold and weary. But on the day of the race, because I had stuck to my training, even when it was difficult, I was able to run with endurance. My legs felt renewed and energized. When the finish line came, I felt overjoyed and victorious. It is the same in life. On any given day we may find ourselves against the wind, getting push back from various obstacles. We may find ourselves being rained on with an unexpected diagnosis or a break in a relationship. We may face a day when we just don't feel like getting out of bed, tired and exhausted of life's circumstances. *But God.* Isaiah tells us in these passages God will renew our tiredness. He will lift us up and strengthen us so we can soar. It may not be at a run pace, but he will make sure that even when we have to walk, we will not faint with weariness. We may experience this weariness, but God never does.

The everlasting God, the Creator of the ends of the earth, the God who has no equal loves us infinitely. He always has his eyes on us no matter where we go and when needed, he strengthens us, and he increases our power. When our hope is anchored in God's love, our vessels will have all the power needed on our long journey to get us home.

There is no other that can secure us in whatever kind of water we are traveling through. When we safely reach our final destination in paradise, the hope we have carried for so long will not be necessary anymore, because the paradise we have hoped for will be the eternal reality in which we now live. No more faith needed because Christ's promise will be fulfilled. The journey will be finished!

My prayer for you is that before you set sail today, you will invite Jesus into your heart to become your stronghold, your Savior, and your anchor. Sit in the chair of his promises to save. Set your course so your compass, (the compass of your vessel, USS (insert your name) is pointing toward your home in paradise and rejoice in the waters you experience along the way, they are preparing you for your arrival at your eternal port. Whether the waters be smooth or stormy, still or sitting in dry-dock, you now have an anchor you can have confidence in as you make your way toward home.

What a day it will be when we all arrive there and drop our anchors for the last time! Now that is a party to be excited about!

JOHN 14:1-4 (NIV)

"Do not let your hearts be troubled. Trust in God;
trust also in me. In my Father's house are many
rooms; if it were not so, I would have told you.
I am going there to prepare a place for you. And if I
go and prepare a Place for you, I will come back
and take you to be with me that you also
may be where I am. You know the way to the place
where I am going."

PERSONAL REFLECTION

CHAPTER 1

1. Is there a difficult circumstance you are currently facing? If so, what is it?

2. What is it about this circumstance that has you bracing yourself for rough water?

3. What do you currently anchor yourself to in order to get through your difficulties?

4. What do you know about God to be true?

CHAPTER 2

1. What concerns do you currently have about a problem you are facing?

2. Have you prayed to God for solutions? Is it possible a solution is waiting for you to see it? Look closely! (Remember, God's plan may not be your plan.)

3. Consider what the Christmas Story has to do with you. Where do you fit in it?

4. Is there still a divide between you and God? If so, what do you see as the solution?

CHAPTER 3

1. What causes you to doubt God when the waters in your life rise?

2. Describe what it is that you are putting your faith and trust in each day as you journey through life.

3. Do you try to create faith on your own? How?

4. Is there a time in your life when you felt God was teaching you about faith and trust? When?

CHAPTER 4

1. Have you ever failed to have your anchor dropped and secured in God's love?

What happened?

2. If you are experiencing a storm right now, are you able to be joyful?

3. Write out James 1:2-4 on a card and keep it where you can see it. Pray. God will help you feel joy in what he will accomplish through this storm.

CHAPTER 5

Write about a time when you felt content with your life.

2. Make a list of all the things God has done for you and given you in your life so far. This gives you a history of God's grace and blessings you can recount when your seas begin to build.

3. What do you need to do to make sure your anchor is in good working order?

4. Do your priorities need to change? If so, how?

CHAPTER 6

1. Are there areas in your life you know need to be pruned? What are they?

2. Has God ever put you in a "dry-docked" state? How did you feel when you were there?

3. What work was being done in your "dry-dock" period?

4. How has your faith grown since?

CHAPTER 7

1. High seas are hard and are typically devastating. Are you currently trying to navigate and survive a storm like this? Write about it now.

2. Where are your eyes fixed? Are they watching the waters rise and spill into your ship or are they on your anchor, Jesus Christ, who saves?

Write out the Scripture verses in this chapter to help you get your eyes where they belong. I am praying for you!

3. What has God promised?

CHAPTER 8

1. Is God making you wait? What have you been praying about?

2. What are you finding hard about waiting? Can you hear the whispers of Satan? What are they? Expose his lies!

3. What story has God written in your life that you can share with others?

CHAPTER 9

1. Have you ever had the courage to step out of your comfort zone to complete a task God has laid before you?

Write about it. If not, pray that he will give you the courage to do so.

2. Have you ever stepped out in faith and been met with crushing rejection?

Could you still feel Jesus with you? What happened?

3. Write about a time when you felt the joy of doing something good for God that came out of the love he gives you.

4. What master are you serving? Which direction is your compass pointing?

CHAPTER 10

1. What is it that frightens you the most about your future?

2. When you die, are you sure of your place in eternity? What "home" do you think you are journeying toward? What family line will you reside in?

3. Based on the information written in this chapter (and the others), write out a "pros & cons" list for each of the two eternal homes mentioned.

4. What will your decision be? I am praying for you to choose life!

INVITATION TO PRAY

If you've never invited Christ into your life so you can have a sure and firm anchor, I invite you to pray this simple prayer asking Jesus to come and give you his grace.

"God, I know I have done some pretty bad things in my life, things I know you don't approve of and I am deserving of your punishment. But Jesus Christ took the punishment I deserve so that through faith in him I could be forgiven. With your help, I place my trust in you for salvation. I invite you into my heart to lead me in the path you have for my life. Thank you, Jesus, for your wonderful grace and forgiveness – the gift of eternal life! Amen!"

If you prayed this prayer for the first time, know that words alone can't save you, but your faith in Jesus Christ can and will. This prayer is a way to declare to God that you are relying on Jesus for your salvation. By praying this prayer, you have taken the first step and now it is time for you to take these words and sit in the chair of your faith in Jesus. You are sealed with the Holy Spirit, God's guarantee of a future in paradise and **NOTHING** can separate you from his love! If you have prayed this prayer for the first time, would you contact me and let me know? I would love to rejoice with you and add you to my prayer list.

END NOTES

Chapter 1

[1] *"Did You Know,"* English Standard Version Student Study Bible, Wheaton, IL, Crossway, 2011, page 1644.

[2] "anchor," https://en.m.wikipedia.org/wiki/anchor, June 9, 2020

[3] Public.navy.mil – USS Dwight D. Eisenhower (CVN69) Facts & Stats, June 9, 2020.

Chapter 2

[4] US News and World Report, usnews.com, 2006

[5] *"New Morning Mercies"* by Paul David Tripp, copyright 2014, pp. January 23. Used by permission of Crossway, a publishing ministry of Good News Publishers, Wheaton, IL 60187, www.crossway.org.

Chapter 3

[6] Gotquestions.org, *What Is the Explanation of Faith*, http://www.gotquestions.org/what-is-the-definition-of-faith-html, June 9, 2020.

Chapter 4

[7] *"Anxious for Nothing"* by Max Lucado, copyright 2017 by Max Lucado. Used by permission of Thomas Nelson. www.thomasnelson.com, page 185.

[8] New King James Version Study Bible, James 1:2-4 Commentary, Nashville, TN, Thomas Nelson, 2007.

[9] *"New Morning Mercies"* by Paul David Tripp, copyright 2014, pp. February 19. Used by permission of Crossway, a publishing ministry of Good News Publishers, Wheaton, IL 60187, www.crossway.org.

Chapter 5

[10] "*Content*" by Vines Concise Dictionary of The Bible, copyright 1997, 1999 by Thomas Nelson, Inc. Used by permission of Thomas Nelson. www.thomasnelson.com, page 68.

[11] "*Content*" by Vines Concise Dictionary of The Bible, copyright 1997, 1999 by Thomas Nelson, Inc. Used by permission of Thomas Nelson. www.thomasnelson.com, page 68.

Chapter 6

[12] Lenya Heitzig & Penny Rose, "*Live Faithfully*", copyright 2012. Used by permission of David C. Cook. Colorado Springs, CO, page 264-265. May not be further reproduced. All rights reserved

Chapter 7

[13] "*The Case for Hope*" by Lee Strobel, copyright 2015 by Lee Strobel. Used by permission of Zondervan. www.zondervan.com, page 77.

[14] "*The Case for Faith*" by Lee Strobel, copyright 2000 by Lee Strobel. Used by permission of Zondervan. www.zondervan.com, page 57.

[15] Edward Mote, , "*My Hope Is Built on Nothing Less*", 1834, in The Singing Church Hymnal, hymn 322. Carol Stream, IL: Hope Publishing Company, 1985.

[16] George Muller, "*George Muller's Letter to a Missionary in China*", https://georgemuller.org/quotes/george-muller-letter-to-a-missionary-in-china, June 9, 2020.

[17] Charles Spurgeon, "*Spurgeon's Sermons Vol. 12*: 1866, Woodstock, Ontario, Canada, Devoted Publishing, 2017, page 22.

Chapter 8

[18] *"Get Out of that Pit"* by Beth Moore, copyright 2007 by Beth Moore. Used by permission of W Publishing Group/Thomas Nelson. www.thomasnelson.com, page 147.

[19] "hope," Wiley Online Library, 1999-2020, http://onlinelibrary.wiley.com/doi/abs/10.1111/j.1758-6623.1952.tb01593.x, 6/15/20.

[20] *"New Morning Mercies"* by Paul David Tripp, copyright 2014, pp. January 14 & 15. Used by permission of Crossway, a publishing ministry of Good News Publishers, Wheaton, IL, 60187, www.crossway.org.

[21] New International Version Bible, Commentary on Isaiah 40:12-31, pp. 1234, Tyndale House Publishers, Inc., Wheaton, IL, www.tyndale.com, and Zondervan Publishing House, Grand Rapids, MI, www.zondervan.com, 1988,1989, 1990, 1991.

ABOUT THE AUTHOR

Lisa Whitaker has experienced the high seas of life as the mom of a Marine and has learned the secret to surviving its potential destruction. As a writer, speaker and Bible teacher, Lisa enjoys sharing her experiences with others as God continues to captain her vessel. She and her husband, Steve, live in Indiana and are the parents of four grown children and grandparents to one grandson. Lisa loves to share snippets of God's love on her Blog lisacwhitaker.com and on her Facebook ministry page—Hold Fast Ministries. Lisa has a degree in Social Work with a minor in Counseling Psychology from Ball State University.

CPSIA information can be obtained
at www.ICGtesting.com
Printed in the USA
BVHW030322070521
606650BV00004B/524